THE COMPLETE BOOK OF PAPER ANTIQUES

The Complete Book of
Paper Antiques

Adelaide Hechtlinger and Wilbur Cross

COWARD, McCANN & GEOGHEGAN, INC.

NEW YORK

SBN: 698-10468-4
Library of Congress Catalog Card Number: 72-79513

Printed in the United States of America

Contents

I

How, Why and What to Collect

"SEEMS MOST OF the conventional fields of the antique world—silver, porcelain, books, furniture—are rather overrun these days by professionals and knowledgeable amateurs," reported *Yankee* magazine recently. "There is one field, however, not yet crowded. . . ."

That field and the nature and substance of it form the body of this book.

The collecting of paper antiques and more recent memorabilia has many advantages for the amateur besides the fortunate fact that it still retains its standing as an uncrowded field. The biggest benefit for many collectors lies in the fact that you can select from such a wide range of subjects and still find a wealth of treasures.

Another obvious advantage is that paper items—valentines, postcards, calendars, sheet music, documents, fashion prints, trading cards, labels, paper dolls, or even comic books, catalogues and almanacs—are so much easier to transport, store and display than most other antiques and collector's items. You can live in a relatively small apartment and still pursue paper antiques in many forms without having to worry about how long it will take for your hobby to overrun the place.

Paper antiquing can also be the answer for the person who wants the rewards and satisfactions of discovering and

VOLUME XXI. NEW YORK, MARCH 2, 1893. NUMBER

Entered at the New York Post Office as Second-Class Mail Matter.
Copyright, 1893, by MITCHELL & MILLER.

LIFE

GOING BY PRECEDENT.

"BUT YOU CERTAINLY OUGHT TO CONSIDER THE WISHES OF YOUR PARENTS."
"WHY SHOULD I? *They* DIDN'T MARRY TO PLEASE *me!*"

Cover of the old *Life* magazine, March 2, 1893, a valuable item for collectors of magazines as well as for devotees of the famous illustrator Charles Dana Gibson, whose work appears on this cover.

acquiring real antiques without having to invest large sums of money. For prices ranging from 10 cents to $10, you can pick up some real jewels. We know of several people with valuable collections who take pride in pointing out that they have never yet paid more than $5 for any single acquisition. The factor that works strongly in your favor, from the standpoint of economics, is that single items are generally cheap, yet each one multiplies in value in direct proportion to the size and completeness of a collection. You might acquire, say, old picture postcards of San Francisco for 5 cents or 10 cents each over a period of time. Yet by the time you have one hundred or more of them, the value of each might have risen to double or triple your expenditure should you want to sell the whole collection.

What is an "antique"? Professionals usually accept the term as defined in United States Customs regulations, stating that an antique is any object of value that is at least one hundred years old. In the more fragile and transient world of paper, however, forty or fifty years of age may be sufficient to place an item in this category. A good example is the comic book, since the earliest ones barely go back beyond the turn of the century and did not really become popular enough to be collector's items until much later.

One of the side benefits is the fun you can have, individually or when you have visitors, reading the texts and messages that appear on everything from old posters and calling cards to railroad tickets, deeds, playbills, advertising cards, riddle books, menus, bookplates and of course magazines from a long-bygone era. You cannot enjoy this kind of serendipity if you collect furniture, glass, pewter, insulators, paperweights, dolls, kitchenware or just about any other type of antique. With a little imagination, you can transport yourself back in time without having to pore through the pages of dry history texts. We sat down one day, while compiling material for this book, to sort through a collection of medical memorabilia dating from around 1850 to 1900. Within minutes we were deep in the world of Indian remedies, Kickapoo (really!) cough cure, snakebite tonic, electric oil, "Pink Pills for Pale People," Canada root for hysterics, Witch Cream, Swamp Root for purifying the blood, Wizard Oil, electromagnetic hairbrushes, dyspepsia cures, bust developer food, and hundreds of other nostrums.

As a result, we absorbed more of a feeling and understanding of a vanished era than if we had read through one hundred or so pages of a book on the subject. The same phenomenon takes place when you collect material that is more recent, perhaps on topics that you would not otherwise be familiar with. Most people who hear the word "collecting" are likely to think in terms of a long-bygone period. Yet this is not always true. For instance, many people have gathered worthwhile collections of playbills and other programs of the performing arts going back only thirty or forty years— perhaps from the time they attended their very first performance. Such collections, supplemented by additions from various other sources, can form a fascinating and significant record of the legitimate theater, opera, ballet, the concert world or whatever else is covered in the collection.

WHERE TO COLLECT

One of the joys of collecting paper antiques and other paper of more recent vintage is that there are so many potential sources within easy range of most people, no matter where they live. Here, for example, is a partial checklist of places and events that have yielded fascinating, often valuable, paper antiques and memorabilia:

1. Warehouse auctions. Most warehouses and other commercial and public buildings where goods are stored periodically hold such auctions or sales to clear out unclaimed or damaged items. Books, posters and prints are among the types of collectibles often found in storage.

2. Post office auctions. All major post offices regularly hold auctions to clear out unclaimed mail, ranging from heavy industrial equipment to paper items of all kinds.

3. Sales and auctions by transportation companies. Railroads, bus lines and others use these as a means of getting rid of things that passengers leave behind. Although such collections are predominantly umbrellas, clothing and luggage, you will occcasionally find paper memorabilia.

4. Property auctions of all kinds. Private homes yield some of the most valuable materials, such as old documents, various types of cards, posters, sheet music, books and almanacs and catalogues, periodicals, prints, paper dolls, and calendars. Most of the professional dealers attending such auctions are little interested in paper.

5. Libraries. Since most libraries periodically discard unwanted material from their files, you may occasionally get permission to look through material being thrown out. The yield will be small, but some collectors have found items of little monetary value that helped them complete collections and thus increase their overall value.

6. Buildings being demolished. Keep your eyes open for news of any buildings being torn down—especially schools, publishing houses, libraries and similar natural repositories of books, documents, prints, and other paper items.

7. Attics and cellars. The thrill of discovery may well be yours in a relative's musty old attic or basement (provided the latter is consistently dry). Don't overlook the linings of bureau drawers or cartons that have been padded with paper. Sometimes you can gain access to the homes of people who are moving, if they know you are interested in collecting and will offer to help them clean the place out.

8. Book dealers. You will pay too much for bound volumes in most cases unless you know something about values of which the dealer is unaware. But look for old ledgers or in collections of inexpensive books (25 cents to 50 cents), which may have interesting bookplates or other small items tucked away in their pages.

9. House-wrecking companies. Some maintain warehouses in which they sell materials ranging from outright junk to hardware, furniture, and even damaged antiques. Root around in drawers, trunks, cabinets and other places where people are likely to have tucked away small objects.

10. Companies that are moving into new buildings or to new locations. Ask friends who are employees to keep their eyes open for "trash" being tossed out that may have some value. This might include worthless stock certificates, very old records, advertising literature from the early days of the firm, calendars, and printed notices from another era.

11. Military sources. When old Army posts are abandoned, barracks are torn down, or military warehouses are stripped, paper memorabilia turn up in quantity. You might locate such things as old instruction manuals, recruiting posters, discharge papers, historical records and official documents that once were classified.

12. Corporations. Companies that go back many years frequently have archives which, in some cases, contain items in quantity that the company does not care to store. By writing to public relations departments, you might find yourself the recipient of old road maps, advertising literature, catalogues, postcards and antiquated brochures.

Don't overlook the value of sources of supply for current items that might be of value to collectors in the future. For example, if you had started collecting first issues of all the new magazines just several years ago, you would have quite a few exhibits—not worth too much in themselves, but of considerable value to a collection if you had also added first issues from the past.

Above all, if you are going to collect, then subscribe to, or at least peruse in your local library, the magazines and other periodicals and books that are regularly published on antiques of all kinds. They will keep you informed of trends, prices, dealers and other sources. You will also become familiar with terms that help you in the buying and selling of items, especially the terms used to define the *condition* of a particular piece, an important consideration in determining the value. "Mint condition" is the top rating, which means that any object so designated is like new, has no wear and tear or other defects caused by handling, and has retained much of its original color and finish.

The other categories are "fine" (in excellent condition with perhaps a few signs of wear), "good" (in average condition), "fair" (having noticeable signs of use), and "poor" (noticeably damaged or incomplete).

Bear in mind that there is a considerable difference between the retail price you would pay to a dealer for a specific piece and its ABP or Average Buying Price. For this reason, it is well worth your time and effort, if you want to collect seriously, to explore some of the sources mentioned earlier in this chapter. To give you an example, a current dealer's catalogue lists an old circus poster for $30, retail, the price you would have to pay. However, if you owned the poster and wanted to sell it to a dealer, you would probably get $18 or $20 for it. And if you were fortunate enough to find the same poster at an auction, you might get it for $5 or less.

One last word of caution: Be sure you know the difference between an *original* and a *reproduction*. The latter will seldom have much value, even though the art of printing has been so perfected that distinguishing one from the other often requires examination by an expert.

II

Display and Preservation

ONCE YOU START collecting paper objects, whether very old or recent in origin, it will pay to give consideration to a few simple guidelines for preservation. Basically, there are two types of collectors: those who derive enjoyment from displaying what they have acquired and those whose main objective is investment. One very valuable collection of sheet music, for example, while visually and historically of great interest, has never been displayed either privately or publicly. Instead, its owner has carefully inserted each piece of music in a separate folder and placed them, chronologically and by subject, in a large set of fireproof files in a room that can be air-conditioned when the temperature rises above about 70 degrees.

Like a good, blue-chip stock, the collection will continue to grow in value until such time as the owner decides to sell.

Although swinging a good deal, either in buying or selling, can be part of the fun in collecting paper antiques and memorabilia, we do not recommend that amateur collectors take up this fascinating hobby—certainly not at the beginning—with investment in mind. A few unwise purchases or disappointments with pieces that *should* increase in value but do not can stifle further interest in collecting.

We feel that the collector who displays paper pieces or at least has collections easily available to show visitors and friends will find more personal satisfaction in the long run than if he had dollars and cents on his mind. We know of several fascinating collections that we never tire of looking at, including: old-time advertising trading cards of the 1880's and 1890's, lovingly mounted between large plastic sheets so that you can study both sides; shelves loaded with those ridiculously fanciful pulp magazines from the World War I era and the twenties, which can be picked out and read, to the great amusement of everyone present; a family room literally papered with circus posters and others from the world of entertainment, with the oldest and most valuable ones—some going back to the early 1800's—properly mounted in frames and behind glass; playbills for almost every Broadway show produced during the last sixty years, handily inserted in glassine envelopes in albums where they can be quickly removed and read through, giving the reader a wonderful historical perspective of the American theater; and a collection of paper dolls of many types, on shelves, on walls and in dioramas, each with a suitable backdrop made by the owner to depict the appropriate time and place.

Part of the enjoyment of collecting lies not only in the showing, but in the telling of interesting anecdotes about where certain pieces were found—often unexpectedly—and the semidetective work involved in tracking down some sources of material. For many amateur collectors, it is almost a personal tragedy to have to break up or sell a collection. The reason is simple: Anyone with a real interest devotes time and work far beyond what would be economically feasible for, say, a professional dealer and becomes greatly attached to many of the pieces he acquires. We know, for example, of an elderly lady who collects what she calls "pure family." By this she means old family Bibles, birth certificates, school reports, real-estate papers, records of marriages and deaths and the like. "Do you think that I could *sell* any of these?" she asks with a look almost of horror. "No, I have become too closely related to the people whose names, intimate messages and revelations appear on the pages to cut them off for a few dollars. It is almost as though they were departed members of my own family."

Not all paper items have this personal appeal, of course. You will not find it when collecting, say, war and military posters, maps, labels, match folders, mail-order catalogues and many others. But you are likely to find personal fascination in messages—some hastily scribbled and scrawled and others penned in a fine, artistic hand—on greeting cards, valentines, calling cards, legal documents, bookplates, sheet music, and even in some cases on calendars, almanacs and menus, where dates and events had special meaning to individuals, friends or families.

At the very least, collections that can be seen and sometimes thumbed through are great conversation pieces. "I have been collecting paper goods connected with patent medicines prior to 1900," says a collector friend, "and find that people come into my home and comment on what they see on walls and shelves almost immediately. We never lack for conversation in our house. I don't mean just idle chatter, either, because talking about some of these old time remedies and approaches to health and illness leads to all kinds of meaningful topics.

"I have various patent medicine ads, trading cards and almanac covers framed in glass and hanging on the walls of almost every room in the house. I also display some of these things under glass on tables, as well as in albums between sheets of clear plastic, so that the paper does not become too brittle to handle. In addition, I have books on home remedies, published before 1900, and a collection of old patent medicine bottles on adjoining shelves so that visitors can actually see what some of the products in the books looked like."

The proper storage and display of paper items can be accomplished at very little expense. And remember that the resale value of paper items depends on their condition, rated from "mint" to "poor," as has already been described. Generally speaking, you need very little in the way of special, formal equipment or materials. And if you are concentrating on one or two types of items, you need simpler facilities than if you have a range of pieces in your collection. We recommend that the beginner focus his attention on a single medium—trading cards, comic books, railroad memorabilia, or what have you—until he determines the extent of his interest and learns what pieces he can most readily find in his community and places he visits, and within reasonable cost.

Here are some of the most common products you might need for preservation and display, without having to shop at specialized collector's houses, where prices are likely to be steep:

Albums of suitable size for the objects in question and preferably with glassine inserts.

Filing cabinets (fireproof if your collection is valuable) for the storage of pieces you do not want to display or duplicates you intend to trade or sell.

Transparent envelopes for small items, either singly or in groups, such as labels, bookplates, and luggage stickers. These are readily available at photo shops and often at five-and-dime stores. (Be sure to use wax paper or other stick-proof inserts between items that have adhesive backings.)

Acetate folders, sealed on three sides and acid-free. These are particularly recommended for collections of autographs or signed documents that have real value. They are usually available only at special shops dealing with autographs and related collections.

Frames for posters, old photos, prints, rubbings and similar pieces that will be on display. Cheap frames are suitable in many cases. However, pieces of value should be in dustproof frames that are sealed in back.

Boxes, large enough so that the pieces stored can lie flat. If you are handy with tools, you can easily make suitable boxes of various sizes and similar in appearance. If not, consider converting bureau drawers into compartments.

Map cases. These are almost a necessity not only for maps

but for large posters, antique wallpaper, calendars, newspapers, and other large pieces that you want to store flat. Some are made like bureaus but with very shallow drawers that can be pulled out for easy viewing of the contents.

Adjustable shelves, whether built in or part of individual pieces of furniture. It is seldom advisable to try to hedge on your budget by using fixed shelves, since the convenience factor is high and the cost low when using adjustables.

Desk organizers, which are available at any stationery store that carries office equipment. They come in a variety of materials—metal, wood, wire, plastic—and in varying sizes. Some have only a few compartments, while others have several dozen. These are handy for temporary storage and for sorting pieces in a collection.

Plain envelopes in appropriate sizes. To save money, buy the lighter-weight papers and in quantity.

"Everyday" files, which consist of twenty to fifty pages, each one with a tab. The file lies flat and is expandable as you insert material. It is open on three sides. Buy the type with plain tabs, rather than alphabetized ones, so that you can list your own categories or dates.

File boxes, large enough for the objects in question. Many collectors like these (the kind used for library filing cards) for storing greeting cards, picture postcards, trading cards, and similar items. Boxes come in varying sizes, in metal, wood or plastic, and are inexpensive.

Book covers, generally transparent. These covers are recommended for comic books, catalogues, pulp magazines, periodicals and other publications that will be handled frequently.

Library bin boxes. These are upright boxes, available in different heights, widths and depths—the kind you see on library shelves containing pamphlets, magazines or other thin publications which, if displayed flat, would take up too much space. You can buy them at most large stationery stores, as well as at library equipment supply houses.

These are some of the basic items of equipment and supply that you should consider, depending on the nature and size of your collection(s). One of the best ways of determining what you would find most suitable is to visit established collectors and see how they go about it.

When first trying to decide what to collect and how to store and display pieces, consider very carefully the amount of space you want to, and can realistically, devote to your hobby. If you live in a small apartment, it would be inconvenient to collect old newspapers, bulky mail-order catalogues and other pieces that require a large space. You can get just as much satisfaction in turning your attention to the smaller items, like labels, greeting, picture and trading cards, valentines and playbills. If you have a large house and space is no problem, then the sky is the limit.

But, first and foremost, collect *what interests you most,* even if space limitations dictate that you concentrate on one particular period or subject field. Enthusiasm counts above all!

III

Paper, Prints and Profits

AT A RECENT auction, a collection of dime novels and pulp magazines of the 1920's was purchased for more than $11,000. The owner, who had started acquiring the publications in 1924 as a boy of eleven, estimated that at the very most he had spent "about $800 or $900, including the cost of postage and Scotch tape," on his profitable hobby.

A lady in New Hampshire who started collecting old labels several years ago discovered that, although she had been able to buy them individually at prices ranging from a few cents to no more than $1.50, they increased greatly in value when mounted as part of a collection of several hundred. "On the average," she reported, "I'd say that the value goes up double or triple what I paid when each one is neatly arranged in a collection."

A man who had for years collected antique furniture and glass told us that he gave this up completely when he "discovered" paper antiquing. "I acquired some valuable finds," he said of his furniture and glass collecting, "but it became harder and harder, not to mention frustrating, to go to a country auction in some really remote region and find the place inundated with professional dealers. Then I learned the happy fact that these pros were not too much interested in paper of any kind, so they would refrain from bidding on piles of old magazines, catalogues, boxes of postcards, albums and sheet music. I began snapping up these offerings and found that paper collecting was a great deal more fun—for me at least."

There is one important field of paper antiquing which bridges the ranks of both professionals and amateurs: collecting old prints. Yet even here, you can focus your interest, attention and energies on finds of lesser value which do not put you in direct competition with the pros. Donald Cowie, a noted expert on antiques, in commenting on the prohibitive cost of original paintings, remarked, "Old prints, for long the Cinderellas of the picture world, have therefore become increasingly attractive. They are still not too expensive and should yield high investment returns in the future to those collectors who equip themselves with the necessary knowledge."

A print is described as "an impression produced from engraved blocks, metal plates, stones or other materials, and which can be reproduced in quantity." The value of any specific print is determined by a number of factors, including the stature of the artist, subject, size, age, quantity reproduced, and the sequence of printing. First-run prints are generally more valuable than those made later, especially if the original plate has become worn in the process.

Everyone is familiar with Currier & Ives prints, some of which are extremely valuable. Reproductions, such as you find on printed calendars, of course have little value. Few amateurs know, however, that there is a whole "second generation" of Currier & Ives prints, many of which are increasing in value and demand. In 1930 Everett R. Currier, a descendant of the originator, started to publish a whole new series, portraying events of the day, such as Robert Tyre Jones, Jr., winning the British Open Gold Championship at St. Andrews in Scotland, the Dempsey-Tunney fight in Chicago, and other major sporting highlights. "The new prints, made on fine rag paper . . . by noted artists of the 1930's may never bring such fantastic prices as collector's items as did their forebears," reported a collecting magazine, *Antique Trader*, "but they are worth picking up. . . ."

As an incentive to collecting prints, think of this astonishing fact: Several original Currier & Ives prints have increased in value fifty thousand times! "Life of a Hunter," for instance, was first bought for 6 cents. Some time ago, it went for $3,000 and must be worth even more than that today.

But, to be realistic, make a study of old prints and other reproduced art that you can buy at reasonable prices. You will note with interest, and perhaps expectation, that there are strong trends in popularity on which you can capitalize if you keep on your toes. Think, for example, of the recent boom in popularity of Norman Rockwell, described as "an apple-pie American" and "portrayer of the American dream." Collectors pay high prices for examples of his work; yet not long ago, when the old *Saturday Evening Post* closed its doors, few people dreamed that Rockwell would stage such a comeback.

Do not overlook prints by Maxfield Parrish, another portrayer of dreams, though of the faraway, storybook kind. He slipped from popularity when the dream worlds faded from popular appeal and his artistry was considered too detailed. Yet he has come back in the past, and he could have a surge in the future. Today you can buy excellent Maxfield Parrish prints, dating from about 1908, such as "Circe" and "Jason and the Archers," for about $4.

This is a field that you have to study thoroughly before deciding what you want to collect. Artists, subjects and media range widely. Some examples from recent catalogues and listings include the following:

Hogarth engravings from the late nineteenth century for about $3.50 apiece.

Sporting prints by Joseph C. Leyendecker and Edward Penfield, from the early part of this century, for prices ranging from $3 to about $6.

English engravings by J. M. W. Turner, circa 1849, depicting castles, abbeys and towns along the coast for $3 to $4.

CURRIER & IVES'

Grand Illuminated Posters

SIZE SHEET. 30x42.

A HEAD AND HEAD FINISH.

FOR RACES, TROTTING MEETINGS AND FAIRS

YOUR ADVERTISING MATTER

PRINTED IN THIS STYLE

IN ALTERNATE

RED AND BLACK TYPE

ADDRESS

CURRIER & IVES,

115 NASSAU STREET,

NEW YORK.

An example of a Currier and Ives poster produced as an advertisement for the company's own wares. Currier and Ives prints are extremely valuable today.

Original mezzotint reproductions of old masters (Rubens, Rembrandt, Teniers and others) for $5 apiece to about $8.

Flower prints, dating from 1880 to 1900, excellent for framing, for $3 each.

American scenery along the Hudson River and in the mountains of New England: original steel engravings from drawings by the noted illustrator W. H. Bartlett and dated in the 1830's, for $10 apiece.

You can also go much higher and locate some fascinating subjects, such as a Charles Sumner "Panorama of the Catskill Mountains," circa 1875, which has seven different scenes on one large print and sells for about $15.

Many old prints have astonishing detail and therefore are wonderful additions to the wall of a study or office. A characteristic example is a print of Newport, New Hampshire, dated 1870. About 30" x 24" in size, it has hundreds of homes, public buildings, factories, streets, carriages, people and topographical elements, many of them identified on the print or in the caption below. This was purchased for $390 from a dealer. Yet because of its mint condition it will probably be worth twice that amount within a few years. In the meantime, hanging in a frame suitable to the period over the fireplace of a home near Newport, it serves as an endless object of scrutiny and topic of conversation.

Because of the enormous and continuous popularity of Currier & Ives through the years, many other noted lithographers who published between 1820 and the end of the nineteenth century have been all but overlooked, except by a small group of knowledgeable collectors. If you find this field of interest, look for examples of the work of the Kelloggs of Hartford, the Pendletons of Boston, Sarony and the Endicotts of New York City and Duval of Philadelphia. These firms were at one time or another, especially between 1821 and 1880, important competitors of Currier & Ives and of each other.

As for specializing in subject areas, you can locate prints of almost any outstanding event in American history, as well as

The dreamlike quality of Maxfield Parrish's works is shown in this illustration, printed in color and used as a frontispiece in *Scribner's*, 1903.

An elaborately detailed steel engraving executed by Illman Brothers, which appeared in *Godey's Lady's Book* in December, 1868.

famous personalities, sports, inventions, local scenes, boating, towns and cities, and wildlife—to name just a few.

Prior to the American Revolution, there were some twenty firms known to have produced prints in the Colonies and at least six more during the Revolution. Between 1785 and 1850 we have records showing more than two hundred and fifty such firms in business, supplying families, businesses, government agencies, the military and many other markets. You will find among the outstanding names not only the ones mentioned above but Foster, Burgis, DeBruhls, Claypoole, Copley, Dawkins, Emmes, Hurd and Pelham. In some periods, such as during the Revolution and the War of 1812, these firms were commissioned to commemorate in prints the outstanding battles, military figures and vessels of war. Engravings of the earlier schools were often printed in one color and then hand-colored, especially if they were aquatints (a process invented around 1750 in which plates are covered with porous material through which acid penetrates to pockmark the metal). When printed in colors, the colors were rubbed into the plate wherever they were to appear in the print. As you can imagine, the very nature of this method makes such plates more valuable than ones that can be mass-produced.

Old prints appeal to the collector and noncollector alike. And since they are equally at home in modest homes and stately mansions, they are among the most useful and well displayed of all paper antiques. We have used the term "print" here rather loosely to describe a number of processes, including metal and wood engraving, etching, woodcutting, lithography, aquatints, and mezzotints. You can easily locate volumes in libraries and bookstores which will give you detailed information on the various media. Your sources of supply are many, such as secondhand book stores, rare book stores, antique shops, auctions, art galleries, mail-order catalogues and the attics of relatives and friends.

As a rule, the beginner should avoid Currier & Ives, John Audubon and Frederic Remington, unless he has substantial

A Remington print of "The Scout" was featured in *Scribner's* in 1902.

Another fine steel engraving from *Godey's* July, 1968, issue. It was entitled "The Lesson."

amounts of money to invest and the time to study potential purchases—much as he might do financial research on blue-chip securities.

The restoration and care of prints sometimes requires expert advice. If you acquire colored prints, such as mezzotints or colored lithographs—and especially ones that are very old—avoid any cleaning methods that involve bleaches, solvents or other strong chemicals. Damage might not be immediately apparent after cleaning, but the colors will eventually suffer and the print so treated will decrease in value considerably.

You will sometimes find a good buy in an uncolored steel engraving or etching because it has become discolored or stained. In this case, a bleach may be used in small amounts. Test the edges of the print first (or a section that is less noticeable, or even the back of the print). Then let the print sit for several days before proceeding, long enough to determine whether the bleach used is too strong.

Another satisfactory method, used when there is mild discoloration, is this: Place the entire print in a shallow tray and cover it with a quarter inch (no more) of clean water. Place the tray in direct sunlight on a warm day for several hours. Make certain that the water is replaced as it evaporates so that at no time is an uncovered portion of the print exposed. Then dry the print by placing it between two large sheets of clean, white blotting paper and pressing it with a warm (not too hot) iron.

Often you will find old engravings that are stained with mold. This is the same kind of fungus growth that attacks old books left in places where the humidity is too high. Using a very soft brush, spread a solution containing equal parts of alcohol and hydrogen peroxide over the surface where the stain appears. Repeat the process several times and then rinse the print in clean running water for about twenty minutes. Handle the print very carefully during this treatment because it is highly susceptible to tears.

Stubborn, deep stains are more difficult to eradicate. Yet they may often be removed by using an undiluted solution of hydrogen peroxide for a few minutes, trying longer periods if necessary. Make certain that the solution is not acidic by checking it with litmus paper. If it is acidic, a few drops of regular household ammonia will correct the situation. Do not use this process at a temperature higher than 80° F. and *never* use it on prints that are colored.

Other stains that can be removed are from grease caused by animal fats (use benzine or spot remover), vegetable grease (aceton), and ink (10 percent, by weight, of oxalic acid in water).

Thorough rinsing in water must follow all treatments.

SILHOUETTES

Many collectors of old prints also become interested in silhouettes not because there is any connection between the two, but because the sources and the dates of popularity are somewhat parallel. Before the days of commercial photography, many artists specialized in painting either large portraits or miniatures. But the prices were too steep for many would-be purchasers, and so they scaled their budget down to the next best thing: the silhouette. The professional cutter of silhouettes, otherwise known as the silhouettist or sometimes shadowgraphist, was adept with the shears and an artist in his own right. Many became famous in their day.

The term originated with Étienne de Silhouette, a French politician. Not an artist himself, he was noted for his extremes of budget cutting and thus was compared to the artists who resorted to knife and scissors rather than the brush and palette to provide wares at low cost.

Silhouettes were at the height of their popularity from about 1750, when they first came into vogue, until the middle of the next century. The simplest, least expensive form was nothing more than a straight cutting in black paper, which was then pasted on a white background and framed. Others were painted in black, sometimes with tones of gray, and occasionally embellished with gold or tinsel. A more costly type was painted on the inside of a convex glass in such a manner as to cast a silhouette shadow on a white background.

Would-be collectors need not be concerned that they are limiting themselves to portraits. The art of the silhouette broadened to include family groups, sporting scenes, landscapes, wildlife, historical events and other subjects, many of them intricate and remarkable in detail. The work of the professional silhouettist is generally of greatest value. Yet the art as practiced by amateurs, from the youngest schoolchildren to elderly hobbyists, produced some valuable "primitives," which are not easy to come by.

You will find the pickings relatively small for objects produced after 1865. With the end of the Civil War and the proliferation of professional photographers who had to turn from wartime picture making to peaceful pursuits, the silhouette faded from the scene and the camera lens took over.

These silhouettes, circa 1930, are representative of this popular art form.

The foremost American silhouettist was William H. Brown, whose work is valuable and eagerly sought by collectors. Another name to look for is that of a Frenchman, Auguste Édouart, who came to America and was Brown's chief rival. Yet, interestingly enough, these two men had, according to *The Primer of American Antiques,* "at least five hundred contemporaries, both amateur and professional, who would cut or draw a silhouette portrait for a few cents or a half dollar."

As the account describes it, there were even armless artists who capitalized on a special skill by using their toes or mouth to hold implements and cut silhouettes before spellbound audiences at carnivals and fairs.

If you collect silhouettes, you will find that the ones that are dated, as well as signed and identified, are likely to have the most value—and surely the greatest interest. Because silhouettes tend to be small, they are particularly appropriate for the collector who has limited space for display and storage.

IV

Brownies, Sunbonnet Babies and Other Such

MANY COLLECTORS OF paper objects find that they derive the greatest satisfaction and enjoyment from specializing in authors and artists who have particular appeal to them. They do not need to go farther afield than that in the pursuit of their hobby and their goals.

One outstanding example of such an artist is Palmer Cox, known for several generations as the creator of those inimitable little creatures, the Brownies. His creations gave birth to a whole new hierarchy of goblins and elves and added a new word to the English dictionary. The Brownie was a mischievous but helpful little spirit, who at night came out of hiding to accomplish some task left over from the workday and thus delight the humans who benefited by these acts. He derived his name from the color of his hair and complexion and because he was supposed to have weathered all kinds of climates and conditions.

Cox was born in Quebec in 1840 and began contributing to newspapers when he settled in California in 1863. Yet it was not until he was forty years old and living in New York City that he embarked on the career that was to bring him fame. On the staff of the old *St. Nicholas Magazine* for children, he evolved a continuing series of stories and pictures based on legends about the Grampian Mountains of Scotland that had been told to him by his Scottish parents. The first little elves

One of the many adventures of the Brownies, this appeared in the January, 1910, issue of *St. Nicholas Magazine.*

appeared in *St. Nicholas* in February, 1883, under the title "The Brownies' Ride." This issue and the illustrations are naturally highly prized by Palmer Cox collectors.

The appearance of the Brownies in book form took place in 1887, when *The Brownies: Their Book* was published. This first edition, in fine condition, is worth at least $200 today. *The Brownies at Home,* his second book, published in 1893, is worth more than $100; while a third book, *The Brownies Around the World,* 1894, has a value of about $85. This indicates something about the nature of collecting paper antiques and evaluating their worth. It is not unusual to find fine collections whose values increase 20 percent or more each year. The market is especially strong today, so the collector who keeps his eyes open and who studies periodicals and other sources of information stands a good chance to profit by his investments. Knowing, for example, that works about the

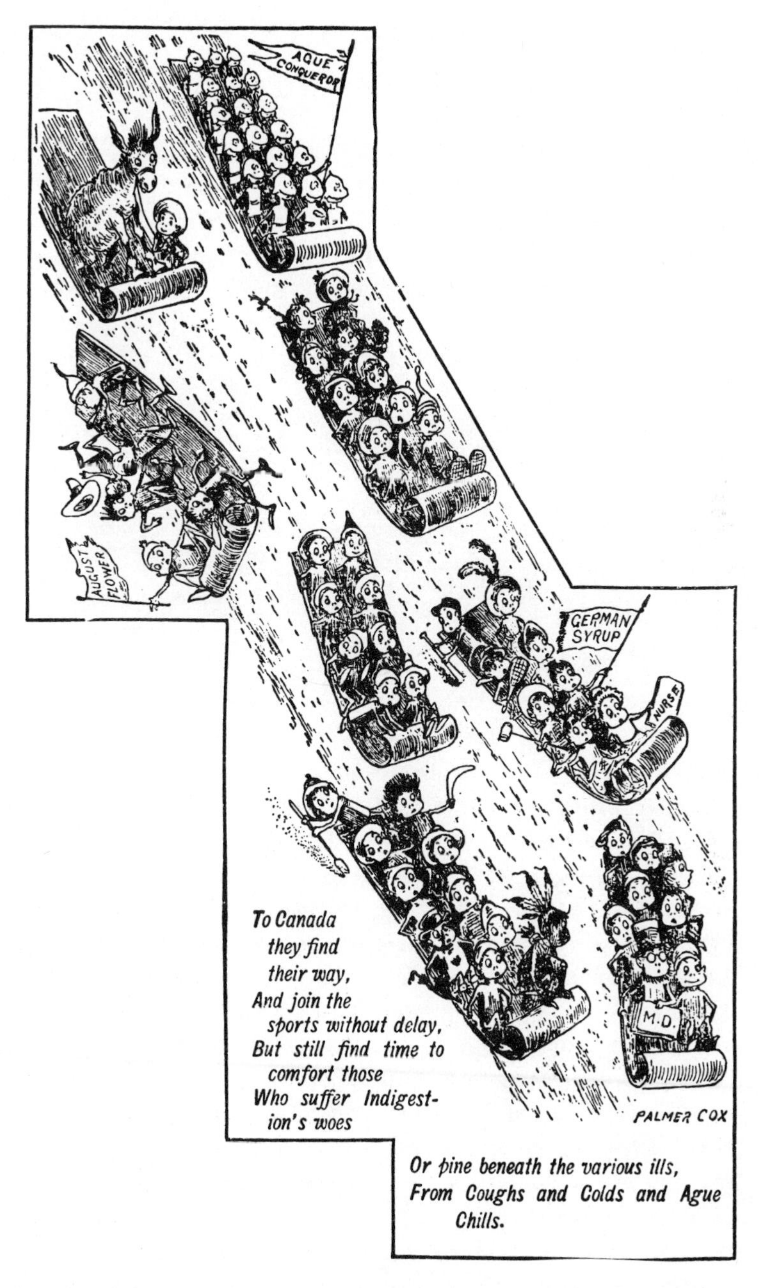

The Greenies tobogganing on behalf of Green's German Syrup. They carry banners proclaiming the name of the product and its properties as an "Ague Conqueror."

Brownies are values makes it more likely that astute collectors will locate new finds as they scout around.

The Brownies were among the first popular characters to find their way into other graphic expressions. They were printed on muslin sheets, for example, in the form of dolls, were used as cutouts, and had numerous applications in the world of advertising. Commissioned in 1890 to create art for an almanac to be distributed by G. G. Green, manufacturers of patent medicines, Cox depicted the same little elves on a worldwide tour on behalf of the advertiser's major product, German Syrup. Appropriately enough, and perhaps not really wanting to commercialize the Brownie name, he called them Greenies.

A characteristic sketch shows several dozen of the little figures on enormous toboggans, banners flying, sliding down a steep hill. Caption:

> To Canada they find their way,
> And join the sports without delay,
> But still find time to comfort those
> Who suffer indigestion's woes
> Or pine beneath the various ills,
> From Coughs and Colds and Ague Chills.

Cox was also renowned as an illustrator of humorous, rumpled-looking animal figures, particularly bears and foxes. These accompanied magazine articles and were also used to promote products ranging from Tarrant's Effervescent Seltzer Aperient to Ivory Soap.

Cox's Brownies, though, had special appeal because it was heartwarming to read about their exploits, humorous to learn about some of their misadventures, and very easy to relate to the different personalities. Cox seldom produced a sketch that did not include at least three or four dozen Brownies, and some illustrations showed literally hundreds. Readers, adults and children alike, had their favorite characters, which ranged

A Palmer Cox menagerie was featured in this early advertisement for Remington typewriters.

almost inevitably in each scene from policemen to firemen, Irishmen, doctors, nurses, Indians, Chinese, dudes, cowboys, soldiers, and even Uncle Sam. They were easily identifiable, yet all had similar physical features: rotund paunches, spindly legs and pointed toes. "Their world," said the biography of the author in *American Authors 1600-1800,* "is one of no pain, no crime and all laughter." Cox insisted to his publisher that he would not portray his creations without having them "do good, just for the sake of doing good, and not for the sake of any reward."

There was hardly a place in the world that the Brownies did not eventually visit, and few popular activities which did not at one time or another hold their attention. In books and articles, they were described as skating, touring American historical monuments, gathering honey, trying to play lawn tennis, riding horses, learning baseball, canoeing, celebrating the Fourth of July, flying kites, going to school, shooting bows and arrows, swimming, fishing, suffering shipwreck, and attending a quilting bee.

Aficionados of Coxiana say that part of the fascination lies in the several talents of the man as illustrator, storyteller, poet, humorist and advertising genius. Despite his many talents and prolific creations in each field, Palmer Cox originals are rare and even his published material is increasingly difficult to locate.

Among other popular artists of their era were Bertha L. Corbett and Kate Greenaway. Miss Corbett was a young artist who, in the late 1890's, created the Sunbonnet Babies, which had wide appeal. These were little children in long skirts and huge bonnets (hence the name). They had one unusual characteristic: The artist drew them without faces to prove that character and feelings could be expressed without using the trite eye and mouth symbols that had become so evident in the cartoon figures of the day.

The children were popularized in a small book, *Sunbonnet Babies,* illustrated by Miss Corbett, with a text by Eulalie Osgood Grover, and published in 1900. The book is rare and is valued at about $200.

Later, Bertha Corbett produced a series of oil paintings showing the babies at work—one for each day of the week. They became so popular that they were used by advertisers to promote many different items. They appeared on quilts, as paper dolls, and on Christmas cards, valentines and postcards, among other things. The originals are highly prized, and even the reproductions command an unusually high price. A single postcard, for example, with a Sunbonnet Baby will bring as much as $5.

Another noted artist, whose illustrations are still popular for children's books, was Kate Greenaway, born in England in 1846, the daughter of an engraver and illustrator for *Punch.* Her talents were first discovered when she was only twenty-two, doing pen and ink drawings of sprites, gnomes and fairies. Many of these were later reproduced from woodcuts in *The People's Magazine.* She devised the figures that were to become known as the Kate Greenaway Children in an unusual fashion. Before sketching, she produced doll-like models of these

A reproduction of two Kate Greenaway illustrations for *Mother Goose or the Old Nursery Rhymes*, originally engraved and printed by Edmund Evans. Each drawing bears the initials KG at lower left.

figures and then sketched from the models. Her talent was such that no other artist was ever successfully able to imitate her style and capture the quaintness and endearing charm that were solely her creation. There was a strong difference, too, in the way she used colors - pale blue, olive, citron, blue-gray, subtle greens and other shades that she inadvertently popularized during her time. That is why collectors are often drawn to Greenaway books, cards and valentines (to be discussed in a later chapter).

As these collectors well know, but as many others do not realize, Miss Greenaway was a versatile artist, who also produced many valuable pastoral scenes and floral arrangements. She illustrated storybooks, birthday albums, sheets of music, almanacs and other publications and periodicals, as well as all kinds of cards. Little known, too, is the fact that she was a gifted poet, or that one of her volumes of poetry, *Under the Window,* published in 1878, sold 70,000 copies.

Most Kate Greenaway works are of considerable value to the collector. *Under the Window,* for example, is currently valued at about $300. Other works may range from $100 to $200 or more.

V

It's in the Cards

AS THE STORY goes, a fine piece of Chippendale furniture on auction sold at a price that was something of a record. The story (and record) might have stopped right there, but the buyer, after examining his new acquisition with loving care inside and out, discovered a small label glued to the underside of a drawer. It was nothing more or less than an advertising label, placed there by the manufacturing firm at the time of delivery to the original purchaser. Yet it so authentically identified the piece of furniture, origin and date of manufacture that this particular Chippendale find was later resold at *more than three times* its previous record price!

The power of advertising is by no means a phenomenon of the twentieth century!

Few people, whether professionals or amateurs, are likely to run into this kind of good fortune in their careers as collectors. Yet you can experience a great deal of satisfaction and personal, if not financial, reward in collecting paper items relating to the world of advertising. One of the most popular and certainly colorful subjects is the trading card, which goes back much farther than many people realize. The businessman's first advertisement was little more than a sign placed above the entrance to his establishment announcing his line of goods or services. Often it incorporated some form of design that symbolized the business for people who could not read, such as

A selection of early trade cards for household products.

a blacksmith's anvil, a candle, or a shoe. Later, when printing became widespread and easily available, the owner of the business transferred the message and symbol on his sign to small cards, which were handed out and passed around to attract customers.

Such cards are rare indeed today. One that is sought by

collectors advertises Paul Revere as a silversmith, and is probably worth more than $100 in good condition.

It was not until about one hundred years ago that advertising cards included any colors. Yet within a decade, collecting these cards and displaying them in scrapbooks and albums became a national pastime. In the early 1880's, they first became popularly known as trade cards, although there is some controversy over whether the term was used because collectors traded them back and forth or because they referred to trades as a business.

Currier & Ives contracted for commercial printing of this kind, as well as for the large prints for which they are much better known. In the 1880's they produced large banners and store cards for displays, but they also introduced a line of trade cards, about 3 1/4" x 5". The first such printing included twenty each for (1) the cigar trade, (2) the horse and livery trade, and (3) general advertising. Prang, of Boston, was another prominent lithographer in this field, and you will find examples of this firm's work going back to as early as 1856.

A large proportion of the trade cards during the last two decades of the nineteenth century were issued by manufacturers of patent medicines. They were followed by makers of foods, household products (especially stove cleaners, for some reason), cotton thread and cigars. With the arrival of cigarettes as a widespread commercial product, trade cards were evolving into *trading* cards. By this time brand-name manufacturers had begun to see the value of using such cards to attract people to their products rather than their competitors'. Hence they vied with one another to see who could produce the most appealing illustrations on the most popular subjects. Accomplished collectors can almost tell the era and origins of such cards by the nature of the subjects—flowers, animals, children, inventions, famous personalities, and so on.

One of the greatest exponents of trading cards was the maker of bubble gum. His product could be—and usually was—rather low-grade. Yet this mattered not a whit if he

Trading cards inserted with Church & Dwight products: (A) Pond lilies, packaged with Arm & Hammer Brand soda, was number 45 in a series of 60; (B and D) "Interesting Animals" were found in Dwight's Cow Brand Soda and Saleratus packages. A message on the back of card D informs the public that, owing to the great expense, Church & Company is unable to supply "each of the many thousand applicants with an entire set free." Card E depicts the racehorse Nancy Hanks and was card number 47 in the "Interesting Animals" set.

could produce cards that were sought after by youthful traders. Since a great deal of the appeal was directed at boys, the most popular subjects, not necessarily in this order, were baseball players, other sports figures, naval vessels, airplanes, trains, and cars. The Bubble Gum Era probably saw as many trading cards produced as in all the rest of advertising history put together. And you will still find cards in bubble gum packets today.

It is not unusual for an avid collector to own one hundred

thousand or more trading cards. And one collector is said to own enough to cover—if laid out square yard by square yard—half a football field!

Among the better-quality cards produced were the baking soda inserts packaged with the product by Church & Dwight near the end of the nineteenth century. These continued to be in great demand, helping to sell an otherwise colorless product, until the 1920's. They were well printed, with faithful reproductions of birds, as well as series on fish, dogs, other animals and flowers. In numerous cases, some of the best established artists of the day lent their services (at a price!) to the design of cards for one advertiser or another. As a result, many were of real instructional value and were used in the classroom, as well as by Sunday schools and young people's groups. And it has been noted in historical articles and books that many a family evening was spent pasting cards in albums or sorting them out for some other form of display.

As Dr. Leland C. May, professor at Northwest Missouri State College, expressed it, "These fascinating cards . . . belong to a part of America's past heritage. They show a glimpse of the American scene in the 1870's, 1880's and 1890's. They depict industry, furniture, clothing, food, our American Way of Life in the latter Victorian Age—all in 'Living Color.' "

But if you think trading cards are phenomena from past eras, pay heed to an article published by the *Wall Street Journal* as recently as August, 1971. The feature piece, covering some twenty-seven column inches in length, led off with the story of a Detroit collector who was willing to pay 33 percent more than cost to purchasers of boxes of Kellogg's cornflakes. Why? He didn't care a bit about the cornflakes; all he wanted was the card packed in each box and imprinted with the picture of a baseball player.

If this sounds implausible, consider some of the fascinating, and perhaps equally unbelievable, statistics and facts presented by the *Journal* reporter: Some serious collectors claim to earn thousands of dollars a year by running trading card

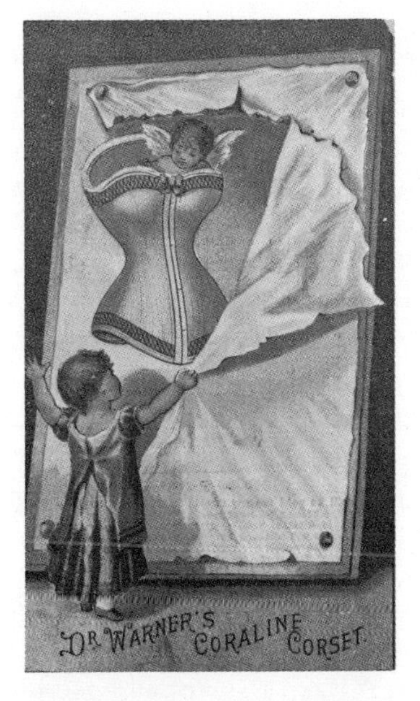

A card advertising "Dr. Warner's Coraline Corset" and other "warranted" undergarments, shown here, front and back. The fanciful front illustration was printed in pastel colors.

auctions in their spare time. They have produced a reference directory, several monthly magazines, and a volume entitled *Who's Who in Card Collecting.* This dedicated group holds annual conventions, promotes the trading card as a work of American art, and has even placed representative cards in the Metropolitan Museum of Art in New York. The collection of tobacco and bubble gum cards left by Jefferson Burdick, a collector who died in 1963, is catalogued, kept in order, and can be viewed almost any time by appointment, "just like Rembrandt or any other legitimate work we have," says a museum official.

One significant factor you should know about trading cards is that they do not have to be of great age to be valuable. A Wilmington, Delaware, collector recently sold a set of bubble gum cards, 180 in all, for $900. They were only about thirty-five years old, published in the 1930's by a company appropriately called Batter Up Gum Company.

The alert collector does considerable homework to find out little known facts about flukes, misprints and disagreements that might cause certain cards to be very rare. One of the best examples is that of a trading card inserted in packages of Sweet Caporal cigarettes in 1910. It pictured one of the baseball greats of the day, Honus Wagner, who threatened to sue the company because he did not want his name associated with the use of tobacco. The advertiser immediately withdrew as many of these cards as he could from the market, leaving the few that did slip into packages as potential collector's items of great rarity. The owner of one Honus Wagner card refused an offer of $1,000 for it.

If you had started collecting trading cards in the early 1950's, you would hardly have paid any attention to the twenty-eight Detroit Tigers whose major claim to fame that year (it was a sad year for Detroit!) was their appearance on cards packed in Glendale Meat Company Hot Dogs. "Collectors," reported the *Journal,* "routinely pay $12 apiece for portraits of such non-stars as Dave Marlowe or Don Lund. In 1953, 70 cents would have bought the card and a wiener roast as well." All of which illustrates that the stature of the subject is not nearly as important as the rarity of the card.

Most trading cards average about 2 1/2" x 3", although you will find larger ones, particularly from the early days. Then, too, there are variations which were dependent on the size and design of the package. Dixie Cups, for instance, achieved considerable popularity from 1930 to 1954 with pictures of movie stars, cowboys, sports stars, statesmen and comic characters printed on the inside of the round box lid. And some product manufacturers have tried miniature cards, with varying degrees of success.

If you look through current lists of trading cards or sections of collectors' catalogues devoted to them, you will see that prices are not high. Many can be bought from dealers for from 50 cents to 75 cents. There are several available on the next level, from 80 cents to $1.25, and a very few offered at prices

Cards from packages of Sweet Caporal Cigarettes touted the product as "Absolutely Pure. The Old Reliable Sweet Caporal Cigarette Has Stood the Test of Time."

above that. On a recent list we saw, there was only one card with a retail value of $5 (a Currier & Ives picture of kittens playing in a hat) and a couple at $2.

But don't forget that if you build an integrated collection of reasonably hard-to-find cards around a certain subject and a certain era, the per-card value of the collection can double or triple the individual retail quoted value.

THE WORLD OF ADVERTISING

The collecting of paper items related to advertising and selling can be in itself something of an education. The early years of the twentieth century saw enormous changes in the American outlook on life and the reaction to the old Victorian concepts. We saw the inauguration of two historic communications links between North America and the rest of the world: the laying of the Atlantic cable and the opening of the Panama Canal. We saw the horse and buggy give way to the motorcar, the appearance of the telephone in the home, and indications that the age of flight was someday going to be a reality.

If you were to collect the advertising literature of the first

An advertisement for the Oldsmobile Model S appeared in *Munsey's Magazine,* March, 1906.

two decades of this century, you would have not only a fine collection but a valuable commentary on the sociological history of America under Presidents William McKinley, Theodore Roosevelt, William H. Taft and Woodrow Wilson. It would include the commercial introduction of the phonograph, the nickelodeon, the carpet sweeper, motion pictures and the silk stocking. And you would observe in graphic detail the disappearance of the bustle and the arrival of balloon sleeves, shirtwaists, and the hourglass figure of the Gibson Girl. You would begin to get a peek at ladies' ankles, would see bicycling swing upward in popularity, and would become familiar with the concept of a piano in every parlor and popular songs to go with it, such as "Mary Is a Grand Old Name," "Japanese Sandman," "I Love You Truly" and "Under the Bamboo Tree."

Loud enough for dancing

The New Victor Dance Records

At last the perfect Record for Dancing! It took us a long time and lots of money. Not so easy as it sounds to get the exact time, and bring out the instruments and notes that produce perfect dance-rhythm, and yet have a

loud clear beautiful tone

Professor Asher of the American Society of Professors of Dancing says:

"I have listened to the Victor Records for Dance Music and find the time to be perfect in every respect, and the records well adapted for dancing."

No more need of asking a friend to play the piano while the others enjoy their dancing. Better music and perfect time.

Between the dances, you can hear the greatest grand opera and light opera singers, and music of every kind. Send for book of **Victor Dance Records**

Chicago—Talking Machine Co.
Chicago—Lyon & Healy
New York—Victor Distrib. & Export Co.
New York—C. Bruno & Son
Philadelphia—Western Electric Co.
Philadelphia—Penn Phonograph Co.
Boston—Eastern Talking Machine Co.
Boston—Oliver Ditson Co.
San Francisco—Sherman, Clay & Co.
Atlanta—Phillips & Crew Co.
Baltimore—H. R. Eisenbrandt Sons
Baltimore—Baltimore Bargain House
Brooklyn—American Talking Machine Co.
Buffalo—P. A. Powers
Buffalo—Walbridge & Co.
Canton—Klein & Heffelman Co.
Cleveland—Cleveland Talking Machine Co.
Columbus—Perry B. Whitsit Co.
Denver—Knight-Campbell Music Co.
Detroit—Grinnell Bros.

Cincinnati—Rudolph Wurlitzer Co.
Dubuque—Harger & Blish
Galveston—Thos. Goggan & Bro.
Grand Rapids—Julius A. J. Friedrich

Indianapolis—Carlin & Lennox
Jacksonville—Metrop. Talking Mach. Co.
Kansas City—Schmelzer & Sons Arms Co.
Kansas City—J. W. Jenkins' Sons Music Co.
Lincoln—Wittmann Co.
Memphis—O. K. Houck Piano Co.
New Haven—Henry Horton
New Orleans—Natl. Auto. Fire Alarm Co.
Omaha—A. Hospe
Pittsburg—Theo. F. Bentel Co., Inc.
Rochester—G. B. Miller
Rochester—Talking Machine Co.
St. Louis—Victor Talking Machine, Ltd.
St. Paul—Koehler & Hinrichs
St. Paul—W. J. Dyer & Bro.
Savannah—Youmans & Leete
Syracuse—W. D. Andrews
Washington—S. Kann, Sons & Co.
Washington—Jno. F. Ellis & Co.
West Superior—Brunswick Co.

Victor Talking Machine Co Philadelphia
The original makers of the Gram-O-phone

This 1904 ad for the Victor Talking Machine featured the famous drawing of a dog listening to "His Master's Voice" in an inset at the bottom.

Two pages of a Star Soap premium booklet containing illustrated nursery rhymes. Notice that the old woman is seated on a Star Soap box.

And, not the least important of all, you would be immersed in an era of collectibles that are growing in value and popularity and that are in themselves colorful and fascinating to own, display and discuss.

Among the paper objects that are easily collectible, besides trading cards, are matchbooks, first introduced around 1892; premium booklets, ranging from nursery rhymes to puzzles, riddles, nature studies, dream interpretations, recipes and fortune-telling; manufacturers' labels; mail-order catalogues; cardboard fans with promotional messages; and advertising signs. The last-mentioned reached their heyday in the period from the late 1890's to the 1920's, were very colorful, and sometimes skyrocketed in value. A Deep Springs Whiskey sign, for example, from about 1911, has a retail value of almost $100; a Budweiser sign from 1904 is worth about $120; and a 1900 Bartholomay Brewing Co. sign, showing a nymph on a wheel, with wings, and printed on heavy cardboard, is worth at least $150.

Advertising can pay off—for you.

VI

Pretty as a Picture

AN EVENT IN 1898 has been of great significance to collectors of picture postcards almost seventy-five years later. On that date, the U.S. government made a revision in postal laws which approved the sending of cards, without envelopes, in the mail at a special rate. Within three or four years, the picture postcard business was booming. And there was hardly a place in America, from the sidewalks of New York to Sioux City, Iowa, that did not have photographers out shooting the local scenery for imprinting on cards, with space for name and address. All at once, America was a nation of abbreviated-language aficionados, and "Wish you were here" had become a kind of national slogan.

The picture postcard was not created in 1898—far from it. Such cards had achieved wide usage in Europe and other parts of the globe, and prototypes were mailed in the United States for advertising purposes as early as the 1860's. But it was really not until 1893 that souvenir view cards with imprinted captions were available to the public and not until the end of the century that they went into unlimited production. These are the important dates and periods to bear in mind if you collect picture postcards made in America.

You will find postcards divided into three main classifications: view cards, greetings, and comics. The first will be discussed in this chapter and the last two in a later chapter,

A picture postcard showing "A Happy Trio" at the beach in Atlantic City was postmarked 1908.

since there is a real distinction. Some collectors concentrate on one classification or even specialize in a subject area and/or period. If you have favorite subjects, it is easy to select almost any you like and still find a wealth of collectible material in a variety of sources. Some of the major topics used for cards are: places, people, historical events, nature, art, expositions and fairs, holidays, commemorations, transportation, military operations, statesmen, stars of the performing arts, religious events, architecture, disasters, products, agriculture, the environment, and comics.

The ancestor of the postcard was the pictorial print, which was attaining popularity in the 1840's and 1850's and was sometimes published in a small enough size to be convenient for mailing. A few collectors of postcards therefore include such prints in their collections. Significant for collectors is the fact that the early postcard was a matter of considerable political controversy. When one William Mulready designed an envelope with a picture on it, he was not acclaimed for his creativity but damned for trying to demean the postal service. In the United States, the attempt to legalize postcards was a controversial issue, right up until the end of the nineteenth century. Yet in some places the idea was met with enthusiasm. The father of the postcard as we know it might well be Dr. Emanuel Herrmann, a young professor of economics in Vienna. In 1869 he recommended postcards to the postal

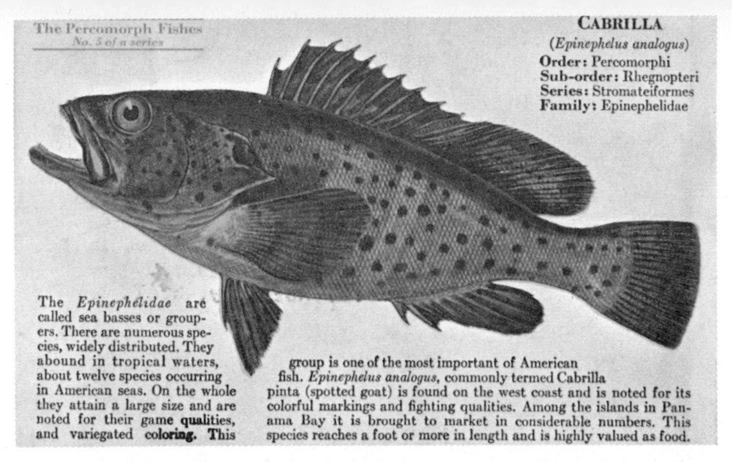

Sent by Mead Johnson & Company to doctors, this card shows the Epinephelus analogus— a fish "the liver oil of which is a constituent of Mead's Oleum Percomorphum."

authorities, pointing out that their use would greatly cut the work load but at the same time would encourage the mailing of light pieces and bring in more revenue.

The Viennese postal authorities looked with favor on the idea, and on October 1, 1869, the first government postcards were issued. These are naturally of great interest to collectors. The innovation was such a success that the records show nearly 3,000,000 of these cards sold in Austria-Hungary during the first three months of issue.

Another significant date for collectors, particularly in the United States, is May 12, 1873, the date on which the United States government issued its first official postal cards. These were strictly utilitarian and had no enticing artwork. Many consider the first real picture card the one issued during the Franco-Prussian War in 1870 by one Leon Besnardeau. But it took almost a quarter of a century for America to catch up, with the issuance of a card by Charles W. Goldsmith depicting the Columbian Exposition of 1893.

Advertisers, however, were quick to catch on to the possible uses of this new medium. The first advertising postcard is said to have appeared in Great Britain in 1872 to promote a monthly publication, *London*. And there are numerous examples of American advertising art on postcards that started just after that.

You may be interested to know that the most famous postal

card, and certainly one of the most valuable, has no picture on it at all and is not really very old, as antiques go. It was an official government card issued in the United States on March 1, 1902, with an imprinted stamp bearing the likeness of President McKinley, who had been assassinated the previous year. The entire stock was to have been destroyed as it was felt that commercial use of the cards would have been in poor taste. But one box, containing five hundred cards, was already in the hands of the postmaster in New York City and was later sold to Booth, Dailey & Ivans, a firm that held a contract for dumping city garbage at sea. Someone with a collector's instinct fortunately realized the value of this haul. Because so few are in circulation, a McKinley postcard would sell for about $50 today.

Other dates of importance to the collector are: 1874, the issuance of the first German picture card, depicting Rudelsburg Castle; 1882, the earliest known exposition card, showing a building in Bavaria; 1889, the famous Eiffel Tower card that was the forerunner of the craze for travel postcards that soon was to flourish; 1890, a noted fifty-year commemoration card in England, showing a picture of Sir Rowland Hill with the inscription "He gave us penny post"; 1889, the Heligoland card that is thought to be the first published in colors; January 26, 1894, the Austrian card commemorating Dr. Herrmann's innovation on the twenty-fifth anniversary of the card he proposed; May 19, 1898, beginning of U.S. regulation permitting private publishers to sell cards that could be mailed at the same rate—one cent—as government cards (prior to that, privately printed cards had to be mailed at the regular first-class rate of two cents); 1902, first "divided back" cards printed, with relaxation of restrictions in England; and March 1, 1907, permission first granted in the United States to use this type of divided card.

The early modern era of postcards is recognized as the period from 1916 through 1930, during which the card manufacturing industry was highly competitive. You will find

A comic postcard, probably circa 1930, of a type still being manufactured today.

that this era is characterized by the "white border card," so-called because of the border that was a popular feature of the design. View cards tended during these years to have a strong market, but seasonal cards were not greatly in demand and the greeting postcard was still a rarity.

During the 1920's, the comic postcard came into vogue, possibly as a form of relief from the tensions of the World War I years and the problems that faced the world immediately thereafter. The popularity of cards in sets and series waned during this period, so, consequently, the chance of locating a sequence of cards on a particular subject is less than for the single card.

The years from 1930 through the end of World War II are known as the linen period because of a new printing process that made possible the production of cards, in color, on a paper whose surface resembled that of linen.

By 1939 publishers were eyeing the use of new color photograph techniques for use on cards. Costs went up, as did the postage rates, jumping in a very short period of time from one cent to five cents. Today there is great interest in what is commonly referred to as modern chromes, especially those that appeared just before World War II. They represent a real innovation and the beginning of an era. Many such cards are becoming rare.

This is an appropriate place to discuss what makes one card more valuable than another. Rarity is not always the most important factor. But, in general, you should consider the following points:

1. *Rarity*, especially if a card is very rare and difficult to locate outside private collections.

2. *Subject.* The demand changes over the years, and the scenes that were popular at one time may give way to an interest in military or technological subjects.

3. *Condition.* As has previously been pointed out, condition can make a great deal of difference in the worth of a card. However, a rare card in poor condition could conceivably be more valuable than one not so rare that is in mint condition.

4. *Detail.* The quality of the printing and the clarity of detail are important. In a few cases, though, errors in printing have resulted in cards that are rarities and in demand *because of* the imperfection (just as in the case of the "upside down" airmail stamp, although at nowhere near the value).

5. *Color.* With the advent of color in cards, collectors became conscious of the improvement over the old black-and-white or two-tone cards, yet without too much sophistication about the quality of the color. Today's collectors look for color fidelity and fine printing.

6. *Postmark.* The origin and nature of the postmark is often a distinguishing feature—just as it is in stamp collecting—and will increase or decrease the value and demand accordingly.

7. *Publisher.* The standing of certain publishers upgrades the value of cards bearing their mark. The Detroit Publishing

Company, Stengel and Company and Edward H. Mitchell Company, among many others, are noteworthy.

8. *Popularity.* Sometimes, for no apparent reason, certain subjects or types of cards rise or fall in popularity and demand. If you note ahead of the crowd that a certain school of art or an individual artist is having a comeback, look for cards bearing the work of this school or artist.

Oftentimes an alert and knowledgeable collector can, with some detailed research, upgrade the interest in certain types of cards in his collection. If, for example, he has six cards using the new color process and dated 1939 and postmarked with the imprint of a post office that did not go into operation until that year, he might have an interesting case. If he could point out that very few such cards were posted from that address and even fewer in the new color, he might attract considerable interest.

You will find many periodicals, catalogues, articles and books listing different types of cards and their values. This chapter could not even begin to include such listings. A characteristic "Topic Listing" (published alphabetically) includes the following information, just by way of example:

Cards showing abbeys, actors, amusement parks, asylums, courthouses, hotels, kittens, main streets, monuments, penitentiaries, post offices, schools, seashores, trees, wharves, YMCA's, and zoos are generally available for 5 cents or 10 cents. But the price jumps to 50 cents or more for airplanes, pre-1915; capitols, showing state seals; coin cards; fire engines, horse-drawn; paper dolls, uncut; and states showing Indian territory.

Artists are also listed, ranging in value on the average from 10 cents (E. C. Banks, Harrison Cady, James Montgomery Flagg, Rube Goldberg) to 25 cents (Frances Brundage, Howard Chandler Christy, R. F. Outcault, Lance Thackeray) and 75 cents and more (Kate Greenaway, $5, Frederic Remington, $2, and Charles M. Russell, $1).

It is important to keep your eye on what individual collectors are looking for, too. Sometimes you can sell unwanted or duplicate cards at a good price and use the income to purchase the cards you really want. Some typical want ads, for example, are headed as follows:

> WANTED: Picture postcards before 1920, especially street scenes. . . .
>
> WANT TO BUY U.S. government postal cards from 1873-1912 in lots of 100 or more. . . .
>
> OKLAHOMA POSTCARDS. Want pre-1915's, with views of small towns. Postmarks a must. . . .
>
> WILL PAY UP TO $1 for postcards using early color processes. What have you?
>
> RAILROAD DEPOTS & SCENES. Buying old ones, especially around Rocky Mountain region. . . .

Trading is very common. Many collectors get to know each other by mail and trade their postcards back and forth, each one thus helping the other, as well as himself, build a collection. Enjoying correspondence with people is a valuable personal asset in collecting postcards—or, for that matter, many other paper items.

STEREOSCOPE CARDS

Because of the parallel element of subject matter and its rise and fall and change in popularity, some collectors of postcards also build collections of old stereoscope cards. These are largely photographic, using scenes taken with a special type of camera with mounted dual lenses. The result, two similar

A stereoscopic view of Asbury Park, New Jersey, copyrighted in 1901.

scenes printed side by side on an oblong card, looks almost like any other card with a picture on it. Yet when seen through a special viewer, the scene takes on a fascinating three-dimensional effect.

The stereoscope first came into use in America around 1850, having been invented in England two decades earlier. Its popularity was heightened when, in 1851, Queen Victoria visited the World's Fair in London and was entranced by the French display of stereoscopes there. The idea of using two pictures to produce the dimensional effect is said to have been the brainchild of Sir Charles Wheatstone, who collaborated with William H. F. Talbot, an inventor in the field of photography, in the 1830's. Improvements were made in the device in the 1840's, climaxing in 1849 with the manufacture of a marketable product designed to accommodate daguerreotype slides.

When the stereoscope became popular in the United States, no less a person than Oliver Wendell Holmes invented an improved holder to add to the pleasure of viewing, a favorite pastime.

The earliest cards were black and white or brownish in tone. Later improvements included hand coloring. The scenes were for the most part still life and were usually produced in sets or

A stereoscopic view of the Sub-Treasury Building in New York City. The back of the card provides a short history of the landmark.

series, using a particular subject as the overall theme. Stereos are of significance in recording the history of the United States and its sociological development during the period from the 1850's until the early 1900's.

You will find stereos designated generally by three chronological periods: early to 1865, when they were still being developed; intermediate, from 1865 until 1885, when they were at the height of their popularity; and late, from 1885 on. One identifying feature of the intermediate period is the color of the mounts used at the time— generally in pastel shades.

How much are stereos worth?

Sets covering different countries and containing 100 views can be picked up for anywhere from $5 to $15, in good condition. Single cards will vary from about 20 cents to $1 for subjects like city scenes, autos, disasters, the Panama Canal, modes of transportation, whaling and battles of the Spanish-American War. Civil War battle scenes taken on location by the famous Mathew Brady may cost as much as $10. "Sentimentals" are not too popular at the moment, commanding only about 15 cents to 30 cents. But if you want Indian scenes, you may have to pay up to $2.50 for a single card; up to $3.50 for early shots of the West in all its wildness.

A factor to consider is that because of their popularity, many stereo cards are badly worn, cracked, frayed, and otherwise damaged. So sets that have been little used are well worth snapping up—when you can find them. One benefit of collecting stereos, besides the investment factor, is that they are *fun* to own. And they can be educational if you have young children. The dimensional effect will hold them enthralled for hours as they relive scenes from history and study the American past.

VOLUME XI. NEW YORK, FEBRUARY 16, 1888. NUMBER 268.

Entered at New York Post Office as Second-Class Mail Matter.
Copyright 1888, by MITCHELL & MILLER.

Life

St. Valentine's Numbe

"SOME CUPID KILLS WITH ARROWS, SOME WITH TRAPS."

—*Much Ado About Nothing.*

The St. Valentine's issue of *Life* magazine, February 16, 1888, would make a fine addition to a collection of romantic paper memorabilia.

VII

Hearts and Flowers

> Good morrow Vallentine, [*sic*]
> God Send you ever
> To keep your promise and
> bee [*sic*] constant ever.

THESE WORDS ARE the substance of the first written message we know of that used the name St. Valentine. It is dated October 25, 1684, and signed by one Edward Sangon, Tower Hill, London. The history of St. Valentine and the custom of setting aside February 14 as his particular day goes back so far that historians have been unable to determine its origins. We do have many records, though, of the celebration of the day in song and story, and it is likely that many earlier messages were sent between lovers and sweethearts that have never found their way into the hands of collectors.

The earliest valentines were made by hand, folded, sealed with wax, and delivered in person or left in some location where the recipient would surely find them. Many of the latter were sent anonymously, without signature or place of origin—a factor that makes identification difficult unless the handwriting can be proven to be that of a well-known person.

An interesting custom of the 1700's was that of drawing the names of ladies from a hat or bowl. Each young man in the drawing would affix the paper drawn, with the name of a young lady, to his sleeve, hence the saying "He wears his heart on his sleeve."

American handmade valentines from about 1740 to 1840 are of such value that many are found in museums and are not purchasable. They reflect the media and materials of their day, including pen and ink sketches, watercolors, dyes, pinpricks and cutouts; on paper, cloth, bark or other substances; and embellished with lace, yarn, thread, mirror chips, feathers, shells, locks of hair, ribbons, dried flowers, clippings, scraps of metal and sometimes even semiprecious stones and jewels. Many love-struck creators turned to cryptograms, puzzles, rebuses, acrostics and other devices to cloak their messages and identity from prying glances by anyone but their true loves.

One innovation in the development of valentines was the commercial manufacture of envelopes, which began in the United States in the 1840's. By the Civil War period Valentine's Day had become so popular in America that one chronicler was moved to state, "Indeed, with the exception of Christmas, there is no festival throughout the world which is invested with half the interest belonging to this cherished anniversary."

Prized among collectors and found in many museums are the cutouts, which were made by carefully folding pieces of paper and snipping with scissors to form repeat patterns of hearts, flowers, diamonds, entwining leaves, geometric patterns and very delicate, lacy structures. Among the best are the Pennsylvania German pieces dating from around the beginning of the nineteenth century. Sharp, thin-bladed penknives were useful tools in this art, as were pins and needles. The latter were used for pinprick work, which required great patience, forming many pinpricks into designs, as well as words and symbols.*

*According to Ralph and Terry Kovel, who author a column, "Know Your Antiques," there is a great resurgence of interest in paper cutting, and "Famous artists are returning to this ancient art form." This trend suggests that there will be a parallel interest in collecting old-time examples of the art.

A handmade valentine dating from the 1870's.

The cutouts and pinpricks were mounted on contrasting paper, or sometimes on cloth, and either embellished or left in this simpler format. Some were hand-colored, especially to produce bleeding hearts and colorful flowers.

Many collectors of valentines also try to acquire the books that were published at the time, largely to help the inexperienced express their thoughts of love. One such, published in the late eighteenth century, was *The Young Man's Valentine Writer.* A later volume was *The Quiver of Love.* Their purpose was to provide appropriate verses or messages for young men and ladies to use in the making of valentines. Most books were divided not only by subject, but often by the calling of the user. Thus you will find verses and texts for men who were lawyers, tradesmen, weavers, students, and fishermen, to name a few.

As a further aid, some craftsmen produced kits for the making of valentines, containing all the elements necessary for finishing, inscribing and assembling. Such kits, dating back to the late seventeenth century, are rare.

The mass-produced valentine did not come into commercial use until the 1830's, and at first most of them were produced in Europe for export as well as domestic sale. A few were printed from woodcuts; some were engraved; but most of the early ones were lithographed in black and white and then hand-colored. One of the earliest examples of these in America is a lithograph published by Turner & Fisher of Philadelphia in 1840. Showing a picture of a young boy, with a border of vines, leaves and Cupid-like figures, it bears this message:

May friendship's constant kiss be thine
From this sweet day of Valentine.

Another valentine publisher of the era was Elton & Company, of New York City, which is said to have started business in this field in 1833. Later, around 1842, the firm of T. W. Strong became prominent in New York as a publisher specializing in, among other things, valentines. "Valentines! Valentines!" echoes a Strong advertisement of 1848. "All sorts of Valentines, imported and domestic, sentimental, humorous, witty, comic, serious, local, and national, got up in the most superb style on lace paper and gold, without regard to expense. Also, envelopes and Valentine Writers, and everything connected with Valentines, to suit all customers—prices varying from six cents to ten dollars; for sale wholesale and retail at Thomas W. Strong's Great Depot of Valentines, 98 Nassau Street."

By the middle of the century the symbols that were to become standard, such as the red hearts, bunches of roses, Cupid with his bow and arrow, and illustrations of churches, couples taking vows and wedding rings, were evolving.

One curious phenomenon took place in the 1850's. A creative artist came up with the idea of depicting paper currency as a form of valentine, using appropriate phrases thereon, such as "The Bank of True Love," and with "Pledges" by the "Bearer." Some such Love Notes had official-looking inscriptions with statements that the bearer could cash them in for affection and true love. So detailed were some of these and so adept were certain artists at making them resemble real

Courtesy, Hallmark Cards, Inc.

A valentine of the Gay Nineties.

notes that the authorities became alarmed. It is known that they were banned in England. And the scarcity of valentines of this type in America today indicates that they might also have been banned—or at least seriously restricted—in the United States, too.

Another noted producer of valentines was Louis Prang, of Boston, who had come from Prussia and eventually established himself in the printing business. His output was small, especially in comparison with the numbers of cards he produced for events other than Valentine's Day. And for that reason his valentines are highly regarded by many collectors.

A forward step in the mass production of valentines came with the entry of an unlikely entrepreneur, Esther Howland, into this specialized field. Miss Howland, like many of her peers, began making valentines for herself. But she became intrigued with the idea of setting up a business of making them, in limited quantities, to sell. At first she operated out of the family parlor in Worcester, Massachusetts, using her brother, Allen, as a traveling salesman. He was so successful in getting orders that she began hiring young ladies to help out—mostly friends who were, like her, in their twenties. Esther would cut the designs, and the girls would take care of copying and assembling. Soon there were so many orders that they had to specialize, using a real assembly line technique that was not to become common in industry for many years to come. Early Howland valentines, more than 130 years old, are real collector's items, as well as remarkable examples of a combination of the manufacturing process and the handmade look. Naturally, they are extremely valuable and would command as high a price as the traffic will bear.

Another publisher of the period whose work is sought after is George C. Whitney, also of Worcester, who flourished during the 1860's. His business was so successful that he bought out two prominent New York firms—partially, it is said, because they were distributing comic valentines, which he abhorred. In 1866 he also acquired Miss Howland's firm and for the next

Courtesy, Hallmark Cards, Inc.

Comic valentines, known as Penny Dreadfuls, originated in America in 1848. This one was designed by Charles Howard and published by McLoughlin Brothers, New York.

twenty-five years the Whitney Company was the leader in the valentine business. One of Whitney's greatest contributions in this field was in the development of domestic materials and equipment for embossing, during the 1870's. Prior to that time, most of the paper lace was imported.

Despite Mr. Whitney's aversion, comic valentines cannot be overlooked as collector's items. They had their origins in the caricatures of earlier times that were so prevalent as tools for political satire, both in Europe and in the United States. Comic valentines were being produced in quantity in the 1840's. A few come from the 1830's, but before that time they were very rare. As can easily be seen, they were simple to mass-produce, requiring only wood blocks for the process. Hand coloring was simple, yet even this was easily taken over by the use of two or three overprints in the desired colors.

Publishers of note in America in this field were Elton & Company, A. J. Fisher, Turner & Fisher, Charles P. Huestis, T. W. Strong, and McLoughlin Brothers. Their arrows were aimed at dudes, Romeos, old maids, sloppy eaters, drunks, prudes, gullible souls, and the timid, among others. A characteristic and much-quoted verse is the one "To a Drunkard," which goes like this:

> Oh! horrid, frightful, stupid drunkard,
> Receptacle of gin and beer,
> If e'er you pester me with nonsense,
> My answer shall be simply, "clear."

By the end of the 1890's the old-fashioned paper lace was disappearing, replaced by a trend toward ingenuity. This took the form of novelties, many of them originating in Germany. There was, for example, the stand-up type, which opened to form a base, produced in Germany from about 1895 until 1915. Dimension was the big fad, and people wanted valentines that could be mailed flat but would open out to form bells, fans, balls, hearts and other objects. Mechanicals also came into vogue. These were cutouts of automobiles, ships, trains and later airplanes, which had moving parts. By pulling a paper lever or rotating a disk, heads could be made to turn, smoke to pour upward from a stack, wheels to go around, ships to rock, and wings to flap.

Although Kate Greenaway has already been discussed for her art and influence on the world of paper, no discussion of valentines should omit her contribution to this field. Her cards were distinctive, yet typical of her other work as an artist and illustrator. Little girls in long dresses and bonnets and carrying parasols were almost a Greenaway trademark. And no other artist could match the subtle beauty of her coloring. Original Greenaways are valuable and in great demand.

Among the most unusual of all valentines of later periods

are those that have been printed in Braille, for sending to the blind. These began with the perfection of a printing process for embossing figures and words on heavy paper. They are unusual collector's items, especially since Braille printings were limited in number for any particular print run.

PAPER CUTWORK

Although generally associated with early valentines, paper cutwork, perforated designs and pinprick pictures were popular in other handicrafts, too. The art, which was practiced by both men and women, began in the seventeenth century and often included numerous other types of embellishments. Among the latter was quillwork, in which tiny strips of paper about 1/16″ or 1/8″ wide were rolled into tight spirals and pasted, like tiny watch springs, on elaborate backgrounds. Different colors and weights and types of paper added to the intricacy of the overall design. Works by French and English craftsmen and hobbyists are considered the finest, although the art was not limited to any particular country.

Because of the fragile nature of pieces formed by cutting, perforating and pinpricking, examples are rare, and those in top condition are difficult to locate. Some of the best have been found—and will be found in the future—carefully preserved in old family albums, Bibles, and other such volumes.

Valentines range in value from just a few cents to $100 or more. Sometimes you can pick up a family album containing 150 or so valentines for prices around $20 to $40. You can expect to find excellent specimens of individual valentines from around the turn of the century for 50 cents, 75 cents or $1. Among the more valuable are the dimensional valentines of the early 1900's. A gold and white sailboat, for instance, with a swan and angel, which opens up to approximately 10″ x 7″ x 4″, was recently offered for $8. A gold steamship, festooned with flowers and slightly larger than the above, was priced at $10.

VIII

A Message for Anyone About Almost Anything

IN MEXICO CITY and other parts of Latin America there still exists a small and quickly vanishing, but cheerful, breed of fellows known as *evangelistas.* They sit in the bright sunshine of Santo Domingo Plaza and other parks with lush tropical and semitropical foliage, plying an interesting trade that goes back more than three centuries. At the drop of a peso, they will compose for any client who requests their services a letter, a note or a card on subjects ranging from love to finance, politics or friendship.

In the United States, back in the last century, there was a somewhat related system for preparing letters and other messages on occasions of note. The business relied not on public scribes but on the publication of how-to books for people who wanted to communicate. Popular examples were *Beadle's Ladies' Letter Writer* and *The Compleat Letter Writer.* By scanning the pages and selecting from hundreds of phrases, sentences and paragraphs, the reader could formulate almost any kind of text desired for the occasion at hand.

Both scribes and books have long vanished from the American scene, replaced by the proliferation of greeting cards created to cover almost any event or situation that could occur in a person's lifetime, from the cradle to the grave. In not a few instances, nimble and imaginative publishers have even created occasions and helped establish holidays that called for the introduction of new types of greeting cards.

Courtesy, Hallmark Cards, Inc.

The first known Christmas card, conceived by Sir Henry Cole and designed by John Horsley, London, 1843.

The written form of greeting on certain holidays goes back many centuries. Records from Egyptian tombs include remnants of formal written greetings. The Romans used metal coins and terra-cotta tablets as their media for wishing happiness and prosperity at the beginning of the New Year; the Chinese throughout much of their history observed the date with inscriptions on rice paper. Among the first such greetings produced in multiple form were those of fourteenth-century Germans, who used woodcuts to make impressions on parchment for the benefit of groups of friends and relatives.

But the greeting card as we know it is a relatively new art. As Hallmark Cards, Inc., the world's largest producer of greeting cards today, explains in a brief *History of Greeting Cards,* the custom was made possible by three factors: "the rise of literacy in the 19th century, the invention of modern color printing methods, and the establishment of inexpensive postal rates—the English penny post of 1840. . . . Printed valentines achieved wide circulation in England only after 1840;

Christmas cards in the decades after 1850; Easter and everyday cards even later."

Hallmark's research shows that Sir Henry Cole should take credit for the idea of sending Christmas cards. In 1843 he asked an artist friend, John Horsley, to design such a card at least partly because he owed so many Christmas letters to friends. Although it is estimated that 1,000 copies were run off, barely a dozen are known to exist today— rare collector's items that have made history. Two of these, including the only unsigned copy, are in Hallmark's Historical Collection in Kansas City, Missouri, which has more than 60,000 antique greeting cards and is probably the most outstanding in the world.

It was not until the 1860's that Christmas cards really became popular. In the late fall of 1862, Goodall & Sons, manufacturers of playing cards in England, printed a large edition of Yuletide cards. Goodall was quickly followed by others, including Louis Prang of Boston, who became known as the father of the American Christmas card. Prang, who is renowned among collectors for his outstanding lithography, sometimes using as many as twenty lithograph plates for a single multicolor design, is said to have been the first publisher to offer a prize— in this instance $1,000— for artistic design.

Logically, you would think that Easter cards would be quick to follow. Yet the first ones did not appear until the 1880's in the United States and even then could be found only in limited numbers. The scarcity heightens their interest for some collectors. Not until around 1908 were Easter cards available to any large extent in America. Halloween cards started to become popular at about the same time, as did Thanksgiving cards.

By 1912 cards for St. Patrick's Day and others with thank-you notes for Christmas gifts were on the market. Mother's Day cards came on the scene around 1914, but Father's Day cards, which followed a couple of years later, did not attract much interest at the time.

Easter, Thanksgiving and wedding day greetings, from the first decade of this century, were printed on divided back postcards.

Some types of greeting cards are broad enough in subject matter so that you can specialize. There are, for example, many collectors of Santa Claus cards. These go back only to about the turn of the century, and some of the earliest and best ones originated in Germany. Until you looked through such a collection, you could not begin to appreciate the many kinds that are to be found. First, and perhaps of most interest historically, is the changing image of Santa. You can tell the origin and date of some cards by the type of clothing, particularly the length of his robes; his apparent weight, since the earlier Santas were slimmer than the later ones; and his facial expression. In January, 1972, John Kaduck, who authors a column in *Mid-America Reports,* called "Mail Memories," on card collecting, listed five Santa Claus categories: (1) full length, (2) Santa with children, (3) Santa with toys, (4) Santa with a Christmas tree, and (5) Santa and his different-colored suits, which (hard to believe) have been depicted not only in red, but in blue, gold, purple, green, brown and even, on rare occasions, black. Well-preserved Santa cards of the early 1900's are valued on the average from around $1 to $3. If you amass a collection of the rarer cards, however, individual values might be much higher should the collection be sold intact.

If you decide to collect greeting cards, it is best to determine what limitations—by subject, period or other category—you want to impose on yourself. Otherwise you may find yourself floundering in the midst of a vast and meaningless collection of everything under the sun. Today there is hardly a subject or occasion that you cannot cover in the greeting card field. Make it a practice, too, insofar as you are able, to acquire only cards that are in top condition. They are more satisfying to look at and well worth the small extra investment.

An interesting collection can be built around cards that once were the rage but have long since gone out of fashion. They do not necessarily have to be particularly old to be worth looking for. The flapper cards of the 1920's are good examples, or the nebish cards of more recent vintage. Or you might prefer to pick certain artists, since many of the famous illustrators of the nineteenth and twentieth centuries have produced outstanding greeting cards, as well as other art. Kate Greenaway is prized by many collectors for other types of cards besides her noted valentines. So are such artists as John Sargent, Frederic Remington, Picasso, Grandma Moses and Norman Rockwell. You will also find cards with texts by some of the most famous authors of the day, including Alfred, Lord Tennyson, George Eliot, Lewis Carroll, W. S. Gilbert, Christina Rossetti, Charles Dickens and many who preferred semianonymity and used only their initials.

Many American collectors prefer to limit themselves to cards that were published in, or at least popular in, the United States. Others prefer going international. Raphael Tuck cards are popular among some collectors; these were published by Raphael Tuck & Sons, Ltd., of London, a firm that was to England in its day what Hallmark is to the United States in the 1970's.

Courtesy, Hallmark Cards, Inc.

A birthday card published by Raphael Tuck and Sons, London, from the "Famous Series" of 1880-90.

Tuck was established as a fine arts publisher in 1866 and began publishing its first Christmas cards in 1871. By 1880 the name of the firm had become a household word in England and was rapidly spreading in popularity to the United States and other countries. It was noted for the quality of its work, especially for its faithful color reproductions of the work of outstanding artists. As a result, Tuck cards are more expensive than many others, but they make for some fine collections. It was Raphael Tuck who, in 1880, established Christmas cards in "the grand manner." He conceived and inaugurated a nationwide contest to attract leading artists to this new medium. The prize money was equivalent to more than $15,000 by today's standards. As a result, more than five thousand entries were submitted to the panel of judges, made up of distinguished members of Great Britain's Royal Academy.

An enormous exhibition, held in the Dudley Galleries in London, was so successful that the distinguished journal *Saturday Review* reported, "Mr. Raphael Tuck awoke to find himself famous."

Collectors who specialize in the works of the Tuck firm do not necessarily concentrate only on greeting cards. Tuck's contributions in the field of paper antiques include, among other items, pictorial postcards, calendars, books, children's publications, wall texts and mottoes, art reproductions, and art novelties.

At the beginning of World War II, a great tragedy struck the firm, along with many others located in London. On the night of December 29, 1940, Germany unleashed a great air raid on the city. The Tuck firm, along with many paper antiques, some priceless, was reduced to rubble. As one account described it, "The records of 74 years of industry had vanished. . . . Everything of importance to the conduct of day-to-day business lay in heaped ashes."

As a result of this catastrophe, the value of Tuck items rose considerably, since in the fire and explosions many old and valuable exhibits were destroyed. Among the few surviving pieces were ones that had been preserved in an airtight glass container sealed in the cornerstone of the building: greeting cards and periodicals of the period when the building was erected; a Tuck catalogue; a booklet announcing the results of a famous Tuck literary and art competition of 1894; copies of the *Times* and the *Daily Telegraph,* dated April 5, 1894; a compilation of signatures of executives of the firm; and a history of Raphael Tuck & Sons written by Adolph Tuck and hand-printed on parchment. You can well imagine that these would be of immense value today.*

CALLING CARDS

Although not strictly in the greeting card classification, *cartes de visite,* or calling cards, are excellent collectibles, especially for people with limited space for storage or display. The *carte de visite,* specified as being 2 1/2" x 4", was patented in France in 1854. Not unlike the calling card or business card today, they are rather easily identified by period because of their ornateness or simplicity, the style of printing, and the nature of the language in the inscriptions. The first collectors were travelers who made a point of picking up as many different ones as they could while touring the United States or vacationing abroad. Some collectors specialize by country or by period, while others seek certain professions. You will find such cards with the names, addresses and messages of famous actors and actresses, statesmen, royalty, sportsmen, and others in the headlines.

Some cards were exceedingly fancy, with black-and-white or color illustrations showing natural scenes, animals, cities, native costumes and works of art. Many were hand-painted.

*The Tuck firm remains in business today, and though no mention has ever been made of the items taken from the cornerstone of the bombed-out building, they are probably housed in one of the company's own displays.

For a time, it was fashionable for people who traveled often or entertained frequently to own magnificently inscribed albums in which they mounted the finest of the cards they had collected. Such albums, along with small carrying cases—many quite elegant and rich, fashioned in silk or leather—are eagerly sought by collectors of the cards themselves.

Mourning cards also had their day. These were specially designed for use on visits of condolence. Similar cards were designed for visits to the homes of bedridden people who were too ill to receive visitors. Such cards expressed not only regret but offers of assistance.

The numerous books of etiquette devoted whole chapters to the use of calling cards, mourning cards, wedding cards and others. They emphasized, for example, that it was bad taste for a person who received cards to insert them in the edges of a picture frame or mirror, implying that such display was what we would refer to today as "name-dropping."

As in the case of other paper antiques, the value of greeting cards depends on such factors as condition, age, quality of reproduction, publisher, nature of art and inscription, subject, and rarity. In a recent listing of greeting cards, for instance, the common holidays such as Christmas, Easter and birthdays were at the bottom of the price list. Lesser holidays, like Memorial Day, the Fourth of July, Halloween and Washington's Birthday, were somewhat farther up the list. Flag Day, Children's Day, the Jewish New Year and Lincoln's Birthday were high up. Most costly were Ground Hog's Day ($1.50 for an average card) and Labor Day ($2.50).

Make it a point to look for national holidays no longer in effect, as well as the more notable regional holidays.

Calling cards often used elaborate floral designs. Cards A, B and C are "hidden name cards": The recipient turned back the decorative cutout attached to a printed card to reveal the name of the caller. Card C is a mourning card bearing the words "In Memory" at the center of the design.

NOMINATION.

At a reſpectable Meeting of *REPUBLICAN CITIZENS*, from different Parts of the State of New-York, convened at the Tontine Coffee-Houſe in the City of Albany, on Saturday, the 18th day of February, 1804:

William Tabor, Eſquire,

of the Aſſembly, was choſen Chairman, and *JOSEPH ANNIN*, Eſq. of the Senate, Sec'ry.

Reſolved unanimouſly, that

Aaron Burr,

be and he is hereby nominated a Candidate to be ſupported at the enſuing Election for the office of GOVERNOR of this State.

Reſolved, That the above Nomination be publiſhed in all the Newſpapers printed in this State; and that the Secretary tranſmit a Copy thereof to the Correſponding Committees in the City of New-York and elſewhere.

***William Tabor*, *Chairman*.**

JOSEPH ANNIN, Secretary.

Two early election posters. At top, the announcement of Aaron Burr's nomination for Governor of New York appeared in 1804. It measured 10 3/4″ x 6 3/4″.

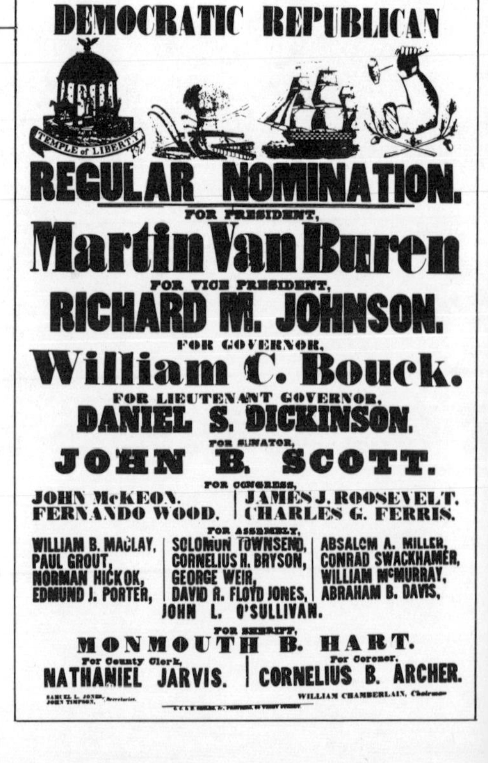

Another election poster at bottom, an 1836 presidential election notice, measuring 36″ x 23″.

New York Public Library Picture Collection

IX

Eye-Catchers

IF YOUR CONCEPT of the ideal collection is one that can be fun, colorful, historical, significant and valuable all at the same time, then old-time posters and handbills may be just the thing for you. Just make sure you have enough space for storage and display, since there is a great deal of difference, speaking in terms of square feet if nothing else, between collecting 4″ x 6″ postcards and 2′ x 3′ posters.

The poster as an art form is primarily a large sheet of heavy paper with limited text and a dominating illustration. Its layout and colors are designed to catch the eye, even if for but a brief moment, and impart a message almost instantaneously. Most posters are used vertically, rather than horizontally, and run in size from about 18 inches wide and 30 inches tall to about twice that size. However, there are numerous exceptions in both size and shape. Handbills and broadsides are generally much smaller than posters, inexpensively printed on paper that is cheaper and lighter in weight, and designed to be passed around by hand to advertise circuses, carnivals, plays, or similar events. They are interesting collector's items but generally much less valuable.

You will not find many examples of the poster as we think of it prior to the 1840's. It was at this time that Europe and America first became familiar with Japanese wood-block prints, which were being used to advertise various forms of entertainment. In fact, Japan had perfected the process to a high art form, had an entire school devoted to the poster format, and was recognized for three great artists whose works were in heavy demand: Utamaro, Hokusai and Hiroshige.

One of the great influences on the development of poster art—as it had been in other fields of printing already mentioned—was the development of lithography. It was perfectly suited to this new medium, since it offered a very simple method of reproducing colors, from the subtle to the bold. Another strong influence was the perfection of the high-speed printing press around the middle of the nineteenth century. Even in those early days, printers could run off as many as two sheets per second, which meant that posters could be printed in quantity at very low cost.

Many of the best artists of the era were attracted to this vigorous new art form. For this reason, some of their posters are of substantial value today, and many hang in our art museums. Toulouse-Lautrec, for example, achieved a popularity with poster art that continues to this day and has been much-copied. Édouard Manet and James McNeill Whistler were among many others who were excited about this field of graphic art. Edward Penfield was one of America's best.

One of the basic things you have to learn about collecting posters is how to distinguish between those from the original print runs and later reproductions. This is true, of course, in many types of paper antiquing. But posters, above all, have been so realistically copied that it is difficult, if not impossible, in many cases for amateurs to discern the difference. Most reproductions will have a later date or some indication that they are not from original printings. Barring such identification, you either have to learn by exposure to collections how to tell the difference or else rely on professional advice. One often has to be expert to distinguish originals from reproductions. However, the paper of an original may have become yellowed over the years and slightly more brittle.

There are methods for testing paper for its age, but these are complicated and should not be attempted by the layman. If the item in question is very expensive, it would be worth the prospective buyer's while to take the print to an expert for authentication.

Because of their size, posters are not the easiest paper items to arrange in a convenient collection. So the best approach is to start with either a narrow or broad specialty, depending on your personal interests. There are numerous categories to consider, of which some of the most prevalent are circuses, carnivals and the like, the movies, other performing arts, transportation, and advertising. The last category sweeps across many subject areas, but you can limit your collection geographically or chronologically.

Books about posters have always had a wide appeal, and the classic ones are of considerable value. One of the first was Charles Hiatt's *History of the Illustrated Placard,* published in England in 1895. Between 1896 and 1900, the French publishing firm of Chaix issued *Les Maîtres de l'Affiche,* a superb venture that produced five separate volumes. And in 1901 W. S. Rogers, himself a graphic artist, compiled *A Book of the Poster,* especially addressed to collectors. Not a few periodicals have also appeared on this form of art, one of the most notable being the British journal *The Poster,* whose four issues published between 1898 and 1900 are very valuable today.

Catalogues alone can command a high price. George W. Childs of Philadelphia, a noted producer of posters for short plays, pantomimes and dramas, issued a large catalogue of his posters in 1869, in which he reproduced his offerings in miniature. A copy of this innovative catalogue, in top condition, will bring $150 or more to the seller. It is said that the great Houdini, himself the subject of many an outstanding poster and a dedicated collector of theatrical antiques and memorabilia, cherished a personal copy of this catalogue.

Circus and theatrical posters are considered by some

collectors the most satisfying to seek out and acquire because they are the most exuberant, have a wide—even wild—range of subject matter, and are certainly among the most colorful. They depict everything imaginable, from the most famous actors, actresses and other performers to itinerant players, acrobats, mountebanks, magicians, daredevils, clowns and freaks.

Movie posters are, by nature, much more recent in origin and in popularity. For that very reason, perhaps, they offer a well-defined category, which makes collecting less cumbersome. Moreover, their future value is well assured because of the escalating numbers of movie buffs and the never-dying interest in early motion pictures. It is rare today when you can glance through a day's television listings without seeing one or more old movies on the schedule.

Collectors say that posters and other movie collectibles are valuable and certainly graphic records of the history of the motion-picture industry. They will show you with great affection and interest posters with some of the movie greats in their finest roles: Rudolph Valentino in *The Sheik,* Charlie Chaplin in *The Kid,* Marlene Dietrich in *The Blue Angel,* not to mention Clara Bow, Harold Lloyd, W. C. Fields, Jean Harlow, and hundreds of other stars of the screen, both silent and sound.

You will find that the "one-sheet" posters are the most common, approximately 30 inches wide by 40 inches high, made specially to fit the standard frames in the lobbies or fronts of movie houses. A popular adaptation is the lobby card, which, as the name implies, was placed in the lobby during the showing of the picture. These were produced in a series, usually eight or ten, to show scenes from the picture. Smaller in size than the posters, they are usually found in an 11″ x 14″ cut.

Other interesting movie collectibles, especially from the earliest years of the motion picture, are the various signs giving information or cautioning about regulations. One example reads, *Ladies Without Escorts Cordially Invited.* Another

Courtesy, New York Public Library Picture Collection

An early Ringling Brothers Circus poster features "the funny, wonderful Elephant Brass Band."

requests that *Gentlemen will please refrain from Smoking, Spitting or using Profane Language During the Performance.*

Wars have always stimulated the publication of dozens, hundreds and even thousands of posters. But not until the First World War did the art really take hold in America. For the first time, the poster became a medium of immense sociological and psychological impact, chiefly as a weapon of propaganda. Torn limbs, starving children, devastated cities and homeless refugees all played their part in graphic art to enlist recruits, sell bonds, generate patriotism, and even to propel unwilling nations into battle.

The enormous and unprecedented influence of the poster during the years 1914 to 1919 is difficult for us to imagine today. But bear in mind that the only effective means of communication to the public during that period was the newspapers. The motion picture was not widespread enough to carry any weight; television was still undreamed of; and even radio was a novelty. So posters suddenly became, as one historical account described them, "a powerful munition of war and an essential part of the machinery of government."

If you happen to be a World War I buff or have an interest in history, you might consider specializing in the collection of war posters of the period. Perhaps in no other similar field of collecting will you find that your acquisitions played an important role in the making and breaking of nations and the history of the world.

War posters fall into a number of subdivisions. The design of recruitment posters became something of an art in the appeal to young manhood and womanhood to take action for their country, whether as soldiers, sailors, airmen, nurses, Red Cross aides or simply civilian volunteers. I WANT YOU is one of the most famous of these, with the long finger of a determined Uncle Sam pointing right at the viewer. The artist, James Montgomery Flagg, borrowed the idea from a British poster of Lord Kitchener making the same gesture. Several years ago, an original Uncle Sam poster was offered for sale at

The famous James Montgomery Flagg recruiting poster.

Courtesy, New York Public Library Picture Collection

$25. It is probably worth twice that today. Another effective recruiting poster, which you will find repeated in a number of similar ways, shows how much attention was being given to the *psychological* wallop of the poster. It depicts a father with one or two children, supposedly right after the war is over, and one of the youngsters is asking, "What did *you* do in the war, Daddy?" The father has a disturbed look, since obviously he is one of the men who shirked his duty and did not heed his country's recruiting pleas.

Another type of war poster in demand— both during World War I and other conflagrations, large and small— portrays the ravages of war and the horrors inflicted on defenseless civilians. Perhaps the most dramatic is the sinking of the *Lusitania,* a subject much exploited by a noted poster artist of the day, Fred Spear. Some illustrators showed great imagination in their art, as was the case in a historic poster by Joseph Pennell designed to help sell Liberty Bonds during 1917 and 1918. It

A World War I Liberty Loan poster.

Courtesy, New York Public Library Picture Collection

depicts an imaginary air raid on New York City by German bombers. So strong was the reaction to this example of artistic psychology that Pennell published a paper on the subject, "Liberty Loan Poster, 1918." Both the poster and the publication are valuable collector's items.

During World War II the poster played an important, though secondary, role in war propaganda. Because of radio, limited television, news weeklies and other media, posters were used largely for information purposes. You will find hundreds of them urging war workers to observe safety regulations, take good care of tools that were in short supply, wear protective goggles or masks, or pay close attention to their jobs while making weapons or equipment that must not fail the troops in battle. A large part of the poster effort was also devoted to cautioning civilians and military personnel alike about discussing troop movements or other information valuable to the ever-present enemy agents.

Photo by John Rilke Bayalis

A 1902 poster advertising Cracker Jack candy.

World War II posters have nowhere near the demand or value of those for World War I. Their role in hostory is much less important. And, let's face it, they just do not have the visual attraction and impact of their earlier counterparts.

Posters do play a significant role, however, in the history of advertising, marketing, promotion and public relations. One story about advertising posters suggests that they evolved originally because of a safety problem. As the tale has it, with the growth of cities and row upon row of shops, there were so many signs hanging out over the sidewalks and streets promoting wares that they became a hazard to pedestrians on windy days. So when laws were passed compelling merchants to place their signs flat against walls, many resorted to a form that later evolved into the advertising poster.

Many of the early advertising posters in the United States were designed by the magazine artists who flourished during the latter half of the nineteenth century. Thus if you collect these, you will find a great similarity between them and the illustrations on the covers and in the pages of the magazines. In fact, covers were sometimes used for advertising rather than to promote articles featured in the issues. Many of the best posters during this period were those used to advertise magazines—*Godey's Lady's Book, Scribner's Monthly, The Century Illustrated Monthly, Lippincott's,* and others which were in their heyday.

The poster is an art form that goes through cycles not only of popularity and/or influence, but of style and design. Collectors have kept an interested eye on the trend that saw the late 1960's reverting almost with a passion to the style of art that flourished during the late 1800's, the early 1900's and the 1920's. Trends like this naturally stimulate new interest in the original prototypes. And so you will find that old Aubrey Beardsley posters (and other examples of his art), with their swirling lines, suggestive nudes and enveloping foliage are suddenly valuable and in great demand—although they may have long been stashed away, of little interest, in the collectors' inactive files. While Beardsley is considered the leader in pictorial Art Nouveau, other distiguished artists of the era are renowned for their posters, which command high prices today. Among them are Toulouse-Lautrec, Felix Vallotton, Edvard Munch, Max Klinger, Gustave Klint, Charles Ricketts and Peter Behrens.

An 1894 poster advertising *Century Magazine*, designed in the *art nouveau* manner by Louis J. Rhead. The poster measures 14 1/2" x 19 3/4".

Posters are in demand by collectors and of considerable value. Some recent listings in articles and classified ads include the following, by way of example:

Buffalo Bill Wild West Show, 1898, 20 x 15	$22
Agricultural fair, N.J., 1860	$30
Hoffman beer poster, 1890's, 21 x 31	$10
Penfield (artist), 1895, advertising posters	$35
Godey's Lady's Magazine posters, 1900	$20
"For the Flag," famous French poster by George Scott, 1917 (rare)	$80

"America's Answer to the Kaiser," 1917, 36 x 45	$60
"Enlist in the Navy," 1918	$40
Wallace & Clark Circus, with clown, 1930's, 40 x 80	$65
Red Cross posters, 1918, smallish	$15
Charlie Chaplin poster, "His Trysting Place," 28 x 41	$25
Automobile show posters, circa 1905, variety of subjects	$20
Poster, 22 x 28, for Rudolph Valentino in *The Eagle*, 1927, hand-colored	$125
Hoot Gibson, 30 x 39, 1935	$50
Reckless, Jean Harlow and William Powell, mid-1930's, 40 x 80	$45
Various theater lobby signs, small, early 1900's	$14
Pin-Up Girl, Betty Grable, 1943	$20

As this sampling shows, the subject can often be as important in determining value as the age of the poster. Some movie posters of the 1930's and early 1940's are more desirable to collectors than circus and theater posters that are three times as old. Keeping an eye on trends of interest is the secret. As the old Yankee trader said, "Buy low and sell high." Look for bargains when the popularity of a subject is weak but future prospects seem good. And, when possible, buy duplicates. Thus when the market goes up, you can retain one for your collection and sell the duplicate(s) to help pay for other acquisitions. This is true not only with posters but with any types of paper antiques and memorabilia that you collect.

X

The Play's the Thing

IF YOU ARE interested in collecting theater playbills, you will find this field a very specialized one, yet satisfying to those with a real love of the legitimate stage. There are some famous collections of old playbills, notably one that is part of the Harvard University collection of theatrical antiques, documents and memorabilia. Other universities, such as Yale University, with important programs and curricula in the theatrical arts also have comprehensive collections of playbills, among other items.

Very little has been published on old playbills. A notable exception is an encyclopedic history of the theater published by James Heineman, Inc., in 1965.* This lists hundreds of playbills, along with detailed information on theaters across the United States, famous personalities both living and dead and histories of theater groups and theater buildings.

One of the constantly appealing benefits of playbills to the collector is that they make for fascinating reading and are, in effect, valuable links in the whole history of the theater. Since they almost invariably contain a large number of advertising pages, chiefly for restaurants, bars, local services and products, the older playbills are interesting and significant com-

* *The Biographical Encyclopedia and Who's Who of the American Theater,* Walter Rigdon, ed. (New York, 1965).

mentaries on fashions, life-styles, trends, fads, music, art and other aspects of life besides the performing arts. Looking back over the years, you can see the effects on society of wars, the Depression, Prohibition, and cultural and sociological movements. You can also see how these conditions and events affected the course of the theater and the changing interest in subject matter.

In February, 1942, for instance, a *Time* magazine critic deplored the theatrical season as "one of the worst in a generation," caused to some extent by the fact that the war had inflicted a "paralyzing effect on playwrights, who have found the world's present plight too big to cope with." Collectors have only to glance through their playbills for that season to determine the reasons for this comment.

Select any year at random, and you will find that the theater programs vividly reflect the life and times and the interests of the public. Take 1927 as an example and you will find at the head of the lists the following light, gay offerings: *Oh, Please,* a musical comedy with Bea Lillie about the Purity League; *Earl Carroll Vanities,* with "hordes" of scantily clad girls in the chorus; the 1927 edition of *Ziegfeld Follies,* with Barbara Stanwyck, "a stunning, crafty show"; *Funny Face,* with the inimitable music of George Gershwin and the dancing of Fred and Adele Astaire; and *Coquette,* termed "the finest play of the season. . . aglow with a stunning performance by Helen Hayes."

Prices for the playbills most in demand are not low if you buy them through dealers. Generally speaking, the more famous the performance or the actors and actresses, the higher the cost. Playbills for performances by Henry Irving or Ellen Terry command high prices, as do those for the various members of the famous Barrymore family.

Since playbills have had limited appeal as collectors' treasures, theatergoers seldom save them longer than a few weeks, except in those isolated instances when a certain play has personal meaning and the playbill is tucked away in a drawer or taped into a scrapbook. It seems to be more difficult to locate programs of performances on New York City stages than in other locations, where a show went on the road or where it may have had its preview run. As one collector evaluated the situation, probably with a great deal of truth, "You see, the New York theatergoer, the one who attends regularly and is likely to have come by many, many playbills in his time, is sophisticated, or thinks he is. He wouldn't be caught dead saving programs any more than he would save string."

The situation is different in the smaller towns, especially ones where an evening of theater is a special and infrequent event. Playgoers not only save the programs to record the event but often paste them carefully in family albums and scrapbooks for posterity. Unfortunately, many such road shows use lesser actors and actresses, which lowers the value of the playbills. Or, at the very least, the playbills are not nearly as valuable as the ones run off for the original performance.

Looking at the situation from the opposite pole, there are a few—a very few—instances in which a local playbill, in a small town, has more value than that for the big-city production. This has been true when a play opened in a small town or lesser city, took considerable time to get to Broadway, and eventually became a historic hit. It is also sometimes true when a famous actor returns to his hometown or birthplace for a special performance. In such instances, as well as in others, autographs of principal actors or famous producers may multiply the value of a playbill several times over.

"You know," said one collector recently, "it is a strange thing that you cannot find more playbills lying around homes. Just by keeping them, you can follow the whole career of a particular actor, actress, set designer, director, choreographer or other principals. Some of the most valuable playbills, in my experience at least, are the ones that for the very first time carry a short biography of a person who was later to become famous. I'm looking now for a first Helen Hayes and a Charles Laughton and a Tallulah Bankhead. I once found a John

Program for the Orpheum Circuit Theater in Denver for the week of November 6, 1911. The vaudeville bill featured Mack Williams and Ida Segal ("Graceful Feats with Their Feet"), Four Elles ("*Danses Modernes*"), The Primrose Four ("One Thousand Pounds of Harmony"), singers, jugglers, a comedy sketch and the Orpheum Orchestra.

Barrymore first in a friend's attic, and he gave it to me for a birthday present. That was real luck!"

Some collectors specialize in the dance and over the years have compiled unique and valuable histories of the ballet and of the most famous ballerinas. Although you will find many of the old classics, such as *Swan Lake, Giselle* and *The Nutcracker Suite*, some of the most interesting playbills are those for ballets which had only two or three runs and then faded from the scene.

The same can be said for operas. But we do not recommend that beginners collect in this field unless they are real opera buffs. For one thing, the playbills will hold little real interest. If some of your fondest memories revolve around *Aïda, La Traviata, La Bohème* and others that are timeless and if you feel that you can really grasp the fundamentals of some of the newer, often experimental operas, then you may be blessed as an avid collector.

If you collect playbills of any kind, keep your eyes alert to trends and movements which might steer you toward a more meaningful, if not more valuable, collection. For example, the beginnings, the controversies, the rise and the development of the Off-Broadway theater is a phenomenon of our times. Thirty or forty years from now, a complete collection of Off-Broadway playbills might realistically have great worth to collectors in this field.

But, whatever else you do, collect playbills for enjoyment. You may come upon some lucky finds, but you are not likely to become rich.

Looking at the subject historically, you might want to build up at least a small background collection of items leading to the development of the playbill as a medium of communication. The forerunner of the playbill is a simple form of notice that first appeared in the 1670's in England. One printed in 1672 for the Booth at Charing Cross is a good example. It was designed not for reading in the theater, but for distributing to nearby coffeehouses and also posting on walls, announcing the play and the players.

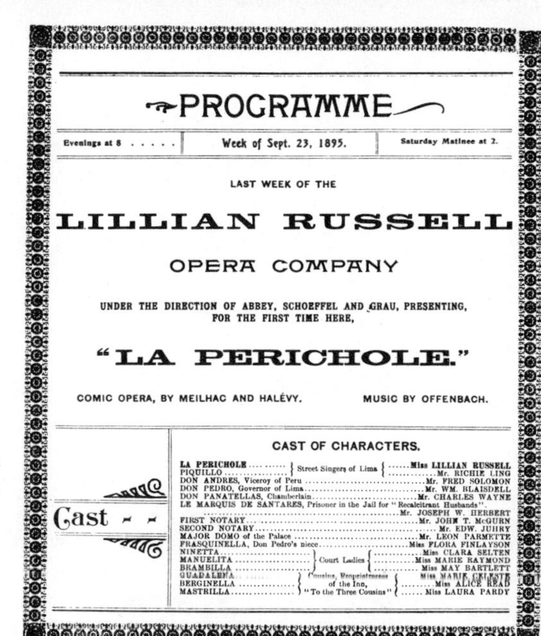

PROGRAMME

Evenings at 8 . . . . . | Week of Sept. 23, 1895. | Saturday Matinee at 2.

LAST WEEK OF THE

LILLIAN RUSSELL

OPERA COMPANY

UNDER THE DIRECTION OF ABBEY, SCHOEFFEL AND GRAU, PRESENTING, FOR THE FIRST TIME HERE,

"LA PERICHOLE."

COMIC OPERA, BY MEILHAC AND HALÉVY. MUSIC BY OFFENBACH.

Cast

CAST OF CHARACTERS.

LA PERICHOLE .... } Street Singers of Lima { ......Miss LILLIAN RUSSELL
PIQUILLO ....Mr. RICHIE LING
DON ANDRES, Viceroy of Peru ....Mr. FRED SOLOMON
DON PEDRO, Governor of Lima........................Mr. WM. BLAISDELL
DON PANATELLAS, Chamberlain........................Mr. CHARLES WAYNE
LE MARQUIS DE SANTARES, Prisoner in the Jail for "Recalcitrant Husbands". ....Mr. JOSEPH W. HERBERT
FIRST NOTARY........................Mr. JOHN T. McGURN
SECOND NOTARY........................Mr. EDW. JUHRY
MAJOR DOMO of the Palace ....Mr. LEON PARMETTE
FRASQUINELLA, Don Pedro's niece........................Miss FLORA FINLAYSON
NINETTA........ } Court Ladies { ....Miss CLARA SELTEN
MANUELITA ....Miss MARIE RAYMOND
BRAMBILLA ....Miss MAY BARTLETT
GUADALENA........ } Cousins, Proprietresses of the Inn, "To the Three Cousins" { Miss MARIE CELESTE
BERGINELLA ....Miss ALICE READ
MASTRILLA........ ......Miss LAURA PARDY

Cast page for 1895 production of *La Perichole* at the Tremont Theater, Boston.

Courtesy, New York Public Library Picture Collection

A characteristic type of bill appeared in 1777, announcing the production of *School for Scandal,* to be performed at the Theatre Royal in Drury Lane, on Friday, May 9. It was simply described as a "New Comedy" and listed some nineteen actors and actresses "with New Scenes and Dresses." At the bottom, the bill announced the presentation of an additional performance that same date, "a Musical Drama Call'd *The Deserter.*"

Not until the end of the eighteenth century was the set designer, as well as the cast and the producer, mentioned on the playbill, although it still served mainly as a poster. By 1810 the format had increased in size, to accommodate more information, and by the 1820's it had been transformed into a double sheet, or fold, to permit room for background data about the play, the performance or the principal members of the cast.

Playbills of the 1850's were much larger than those of today, the standard size being 26″ x 17″, folded in the middle. An innovation occurred in 1856, when Charles Kean, manager of the Princess Theatre in London, issued a playbill that was 20″ x 30″, folded in three parts. One column was devoted to what was described as "lengthy dissertations on his Shakespearian

Theatre, Water Street.

MONDAY Evening, March 11, 1799.
And Every Evening this Week.
At Mr. G R A N T's, No. 242, Water Street,
Between Beekman and Pecks *Slip*
Will be preſented a GRAND MEDLEY of ENTERTAINMENTS in 5 Parts,

P A R T I.

Comic Scene between the Old Beggarman & the Termagant Landlady

P A R T II.

By the much admired

Ombres Chinoiſes,

Willl be preſented the

BROKEN BRIDGE,

Or the Diſappointed Traveller. With the Downfall of

The Impertinent Carpenter

P A R T III.

The ingenious ſcene of the SPORTSMAN and his faithful DOG,
Which has never failed of giving univerſal ſatisfaction.

P A R IV.

A Grand Collection of Wax-Work Figures, repreſenting the ancient Court of

Alexander the Great,

Their graceful movements have never failed of giving univerſal ſatisfaction.
The Performer has ſpared neither pains nor expence in the richneſs of their dreſs.

By the curious Pruſſian Fanticina will be performed the following Figures:
The Merry Humours of Old JONATHAN and his WIFE,
A Figure in the character of a Country Girl, will dance a JIG, as natural as Life,
A Hornpipe by a ſmall Figure in the character of an American Tar.
The aſtoniſhing Lapland *Lady* will dance a Jig, and change her Face three times imperceptible. Likewiſe a brilliant Collection of FIGURES
Being the richeſt of the Kind ever exhibited.
A Curious ITALIAN SCARAMOUCH will dance a Fandango, and put himſelf into twenty different ſhapes, being one of the greateſt Curoſities ever preſented to an American audience.

Courtesy, New York Public Library Picture Collection

A playbill dating from 1799.

HOWARD ATHENÆUM

SOLE LESSEE & MANAGER..............Mr. E. L. DAVENPORT
Ass't Manager.......J. P. Price | Treasurer..........C. F. Davenport

NOTICE!—CHANGE OF TIME,
Doors open at 6 1-2..........Commences at 7.

Second Week of THE GREAT AMERICAN TRAGEDIAN

MR. EDWIN BOOTH

This, WEDNESDAY EVENING, OCT. 26, '59.
Will be presented Shakespeare's Tragedy of

RICHARD III

Or,—The Battle of Bosworth Field.

DUKE OF GLOSTER, afterwards Richard III....Mr EDWIN BOOTH

King Henry............Mr Hanchett	Tyrell......................Mr Otis
Richmond...........Mr. Hardenburg	Blount....................Mr Wilkes
Duke of Buckingham. ......Mr Rand	Oxford..................Mr Snowden
Lord Stanley........Mr W. H. Curtis	Officer......................Mr Hills
Tressel..................Mr Reynolds	Prince of Wales.........Miss F. Price
Catesby...................Mr Selwyn	Duke of York.............Miss Jones
Ratcliffe..................Mr Browne	Queen Elizabeth.......Miss Mestayer
Duke of Norfolk.............Mr. Price	Lady Anne...............Miss Sylvia
Lieut of Tower...........Mr. Verney	Duchess of York......Mrs Hanchett
Lord Mayor..............Mr Lennox	

Previous to the Play,—POLISH OVERTURE..........ORCHESTRA
The Orchestra is composed of First Class Performers, among them the Celebrated Cornet and Bugle Player, MR. EDWARD KENDALL,
Musical Director.... ... .Mr. Thomas Comer

To conclude with the irresistibly funny farce entitled

ICI ON PARLE FRANCAIS!

Mr Spriggins..Mr Setchell
Major Rigalus Rattan..Mr Curtis
Victor Dubois..Mr Reynolds
Mrs Spriggins..Mrs Hanchett
Julia, wife of Major Rattan...................................Mrs Rand
Angelina..Miss LeClare
Ann Maria...Miss F. Price

NUMEROUS APPLICATIONS having been made at the Box Office, to ascertain if RICHELIEU will be repeated, the Manager begs to announce that Mr EDWIN BOOTH will appear in that character once more on Thursday Evening, Oct. 27th.

FRIDAY EVENING, Oct. 28th.

Benefit of Mr. EDWIN BOOTH
The STRANGER & DON CÆSAR DE BAZAN.

During the Engagement of MR. BOOTH, he will appear in several New Characters.

The Manager will not be responsible for any debts contracted for this Establishment, or any members thereof, unless under his written order
E. L. DAVENPORT

Boston Mammoth Steam Job Printing Establishment, 2 Spring Lane

Announcement of the appearance of the famous tragedian Edwin Booth in a performance of *Richard III,* October 26, 1859.

Courtesy, New York Public Library Picture Collection

productions. Pantomime characters of this period were also provided with descriptions of a humorous nature, consisting almost entirely of puns in the taste of the time."

The small-size playbill probably originated at the Olympic Theatre in London, which, in the 1850's, began using a printed sheet 9″ x 12″, folded in half. The Drury Lane Theatre followed suit, as did other houses in England and shortly thereafter in the United States.

The idea of using the playbill as an advertising medium did not occur to anyone until the 1860's, when the firm of Eugene Remmel, "Perfumers of London and Paris," made an arrangement with theaters to supply small playbills with die-cut lace-paper borders and one of the four pages used for an advertisement. The firm achieved special attention, however, by dousing the programs with perfume just prior to each performance.

In 1869 a magazine program with the title *Bill of the Play* appeared. It was like the modern playbill in that two of the four pages contained written information about the theater, the production and the players, along with practical data about transportation, cab fares and refreshment. By the 1870's this type of playbill was also being embellished with sketches of actors and actresses and scenes from the play.

Just before World War I, the 6" x 9" type of theater program became common. They became more standardized in size and design when one publisher—often a company contracting to serve refreshments—assumed the job of preparing playbills for several theaters at one time. The magazine format was largely developed in the United States in the early 1920's and appealed so to the theatergoers that it was much copied abroad. Issues of twenty or thirty-two pages, and even as many as forty-eight—similar to today's—were not uncommon. All of them were well loaded with advertising, and some had several pages in color.

Among the most sought-after playbills by many collectors are the ones that broke with tradition. These include the "firsts," of course, but also the occasional one that made some unusual use of size, shape or material. Playbills have been printed on silk, satin, plastic, cardboard and even thin sheets of wood. One attempt was made to introduce a type on a transparent sheet, the object being to make it readable in the dark when held up against the reflection of the stage lights. Besides the rectangular, shapes have included squares, circles, ovals and triangles.

Look for the original issues of playbills for those performances that were milestones in theatrical history or that featured unusually fine casts or famous performers. These are the ones most likely to be of value and certainly of greatest

Playbills for the Broadway productions of the musicals *Mame* and *Fiddler on the Roof.*

signficance and worth for your collection. It is not unusual to pay, or be paid, $10 or $12 for a playbill of a performance that attracted special attention from the critics or the public forty or fifty years ago, or even since World War II in some instances, depending on the fame of the play and its stars. Playbills for performances in which the Barrymores appeared or early productions in which the Lunts were featured command high prices today and are even more valuable if they are autographed.

XI

"All Aboarrrd!"

IN MARCH, 1972, newspapers up and down the East Coast, and even across the United States, recorded an event unfamiliar to most readers. This was the huge auction by the Penn Central Railroad of documents, mementos and antiques accumulated in its offices and warehouses over many generations of railroading. The auction, which lasted three days, held a great fascination for railroad buffs, who were able to inspect, if not to bid for, oil paintings of railroad scenes, scale models of locomotives, equipment from Pullman cars, gate signs, and many other objects being sold in a total of 1,877 lots.

The event was of particular interest, though, to one group of collectors who were accustomed to railroad and similar industrial auctions, though perhaps not on such a grand scale. These were the collectors of paper memorabilia relating to transportation in general and railroading in particular. For among the offerings were old ticket stubs, informational pamphlets, assorted railroad manuals, interesting correspondence from bygone eras, posters and photographs. Cardboard boxes, loaded with printed matter, averaged about $100 per box—surely worth more than that when sorted and evaluated on an individual item basis. Among the more valuable paper items were two albums with photographs of locomotives. One went for $400 and the other for $600.

Yet perhaps the most valuable single item in the auction, as far as paper is concerned, was the 115-page yellow catalogue, published in 1972 just for use at the Penn Central auction. Some twenty years from now, it could conceivably be greatly in demand by a future generation of collectors. That is one reason why collecting paper items can be so exciting; today's strictly utilitarian publication can well be tomorrow's find.

Among the many types of paper acquisitions you can get within the railroad category are these:

Posters. Many of the posters, handbills and related display materials are just as valuable and interesting as some of the posters already described in other subject areas. The ones used in stations tend to have more textual information, though, than the average poster, since they were designed to be viewed while people were waiting for trains and had time for close-up scrutiny. In some of the exhibits that go back a century or more, the language used is colorful and often very amusing.

Maps. You do not find maps very often in recent times, but for many years city and town and regional maps were common in almost every railroad depot. Passengers were all but lost without specific information about streets, distances, and transportation available when they reached an unfamiliar location on the railroad line. Some collectors' maps of this type are classics. One of the originators of the decorative map as we know it today was Macdonald Gill, architect, muralist and cartographer, who is best known for the maps he prepared for the London subway system, the underground. Early in this century, he was commissioned to prepare a series that was later to become famous on "The Wonderground of London."

Timetables. These go back to the earliest days of railroading. They are of great interest to collectors because they reveal, right down to the minute, how long it took for different trains to make their runs between cities. Recent timetables are growing in value— and will certainly do so in the future— now that so many of the long-distance hauls have been done away with. Today you will find few timetables of interest. Most of them relate just to short-distance commuter traffic.

Tickets. Do you remember the old, accordion-type tickets for passage to a distant city that unfolded a foot or more? These have value today, as do tickets from long-bygone eras that are still in good condition.

Bonds. Securities and related documents, including railroad bonds, will be covered in a later chapter. But railroad buffs often include them in their collections, even though they have no interest in other types of bonds. These were issued to help railroads finance new equipment or acquire property and rights-of-way, among other ventures.

Advertising. Ads and related promotional material for some of the great trains in history are good collectible items, although few have any great value. Collections are especially enhanced if you can acquire sets of related material. This might include an advertisement dating from around 1904 for the famous Twentieth Century Limited ("Chicago and New York in 20 Hours"), a poster announcing the run, sample tickets, a timetable and perhaps some of the office documents on the train that were maintained by railroad personnel. Valuable to include would be a notable print, offered in New York Central ads for 50 cents, "showing this great train, set in a charming landscape, pronounced by persons who have examined it as the finest train view ever issued; suitable for framing."

Excursion Notices. These are valuable more for the feelings of nostalgia they evoke than for any great monetary value. It is fun to go through a collection of these papers, covering a number of different eras, and read the descriptions of the places mentioned, in the days when the railroads extended their iron fingers into relatively remote areas of the countryside, where they can no longer afford to venture. Most collectors complement these notices and schedules with whatever illustrations they can locate of the excursions described.

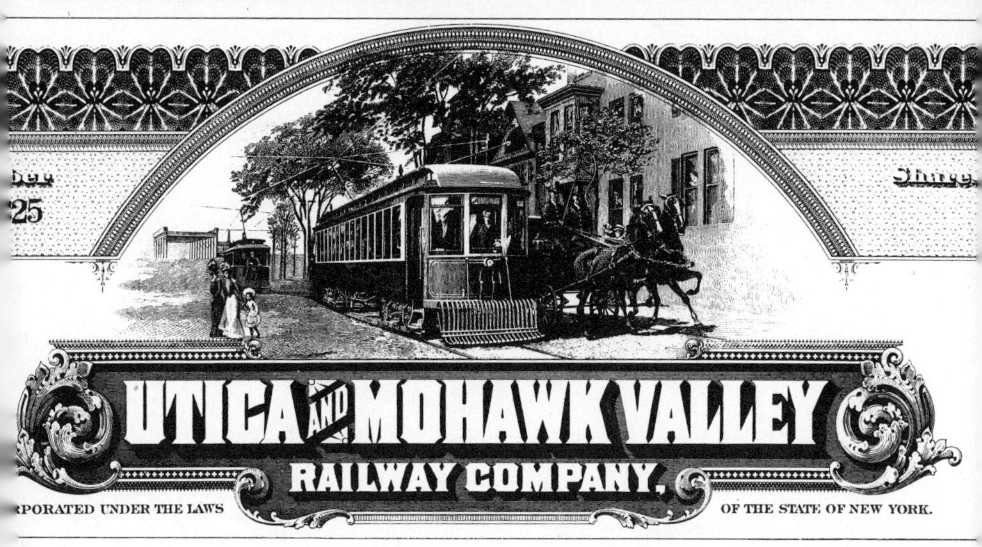

Ornate illustration printed on a certificate for "preferred capital stock" for the Utica and Mohawk Valley Railway Company.

Documentary Records. Serious collectors are not happy unless they have samples of old records, which might include ledgers, bills of lading, daily ticket sales, train registers, telegraph orders, freight contracts and receipts, way bills, passes, and maintenance inspections.

Prints. Many of the finest American prints of the last half of the nineteenth century and the beginning of the twentieth depict trains, locomotives or other aspects of railroading. Some collectors prize specialized prints showing early locomotives, such as "Old Ironsides," built by Baldwin in 1832 for the Philadelphia, Germantown and Norristown Railway; Baltimore & Ohio's famous "Atlantic" locomotive, on a run with two passenger coaches in 1830; the "John Stevens" engine built in 1825; and the colorful and unique engine with a tilted boiler for the Mount Washington (New Hampshire) Cog Railway, opened in July, 1869.

Patent Diagrams. Such diagrams, covering every product or piece of equipment you can imagine, are most interesting when the subject is railroading. You will find ingenious patents for seats that unfolded to form sleeping berths; the famous Pullman designs; catching posts for snatching mailbags from speeding trains going through small towns; and "painless"

A Currier and Ives railroad print, copyrighted in 1876.

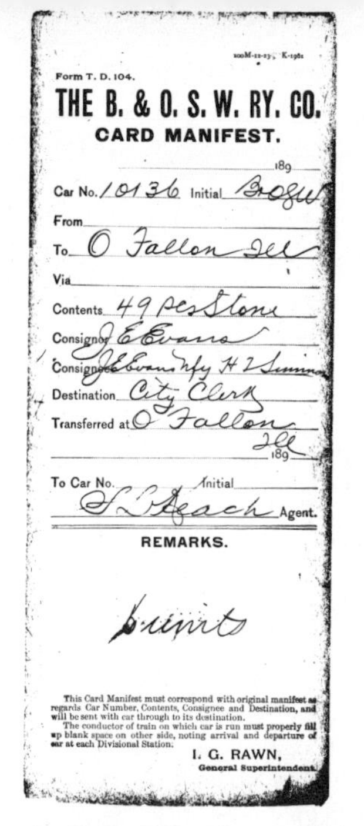

Form T. D. 104.

THE B. & O. S. W. RY. CO.

CARD MANIFEST.

189

Car No. 10136 Initial

From

To O Fallon Ill

Via

Contents 49 pcs Stone

Consignor

Consignee

Destination City Clerk

Transferred at O Fallon Ill 189

To Car No. Initial

Agent.

REMARKS.

This Card Manifest must correspond with original manifest as regards Car Number, Contents, Consignee and Destination, and will be sent with car through to its destination.
The conductor of train on which car is run must properly fill up blank space on other side, noting arrival and departure of car at each Divisional Station.

I. G. RAWN,
General Superintendent.

BALTO. & OHIO SOUTHWESTERN RAILWAY.

Round Trip Ticket Stub. Form L-23.

NOT GOOD FOR PASSAGE.

O'FALLON

—TO—

St. Louis and Return.

ISSUED.................................189

Agents must fill up Stub in Ink, and Stamp all Coupons Plainly

1577 $..................

A ticket stub and a card manifest for the B & O Railway Company, stamped Dec. 2, 1898.

cowcatchers that removed animals from tracks while the engine was in motion, with little or no injury. Because such patents are illustrated with sketches, diagrams or both, they are fascinating to look at, as well as amusing to read about.

Forwarder's Receipts. These were forms used by the railroads to acknowledge receipt of goods and materials consigned to the railroad for shipping. In general, receipts that were filled out and signed are more valuable than the blank forms, even though the latter may be in better condition. The railroads used forwarding agents, many of which have long gone out of business, but American Express and Wells Fargo are two of several that have survived.

Signs. Although most of the old signs were printed on heavy metal or wood (and hence are outside the realm of the collector of paper), several were of cardboard or even stiff paper. These are, for the most part, notices that were placed in waiting rooms or inside passenger cars. They emphasized safety rules (*Do Not Get on or off Platform While Train Is in*

Motion), pointed out matters of etiquette (*Spitting on the Floor Is Forbidden*), or pointed the way to the *Gentlemen's Parlor, Ladies' Lavatory* or other locations.

Paper items in the railroad field are generally inexpensive. For example, you can buy from a dealer the following items for about $8: American Express forwarding ticket, circa 1850; B&O ticket of the 1870's; Pennsylvania Railroad timetable, 1889; and an 1890 pass for the Burlington Railroad.

You can obtain 1850 express tickets in the name of Adams & Company or Kinsley & Company for only $5, as well as several different railroad bonds and tickets dating from the 1880's and 1890's.

But railroad buffs and paper collectors are always seeking the acquisition that is unusual and will one day have great value (even if they have no intention of selling it to earn a profit). Such an item is a freight bill, on pink paper, dated May, 1861, and listed as "Port of Entry from U.S. to CSA." Its retail value was recently listed as $225 and may well be steadily increasing.

It is this kind of rarity that keeps collectors on their toes and constantly excited about their hobby.

PENNSYLVANIA TOURS!

MOST UNIQUE PLEASURE TRIPS AVAILABLE.

—PRESENTING—

The Choicest Opportunities for a Winter Vacation!

CALIFORNIA.

February 8th, 1893.

March 2d, 1893.

March 29th, 1893.

FLORIDA.

January 31st,

February 14th and 28th,

March 14th and 28th, 1893

Old Point Comfort, Va.

December 27th, 1892.

Old Point Comfort, Washington, and Richmond.

February 8th, 1893.

Superbly Appointed Special Trains, in charge of Tourist Agent and Chaperon

xcursion Tickets, including all Traveling Expenses, are Sold at the Most Liberal Rates.

More Reasonable, More American, More Comfortable than a Trip Abroad.

For itineraries and tickets, address Tourist Agent, Pennsylvania R. R., 849 Broadway, New York; 205 Washington St. ston, or 233 S. 4th St., Philadelphia.

CHAS. E. PUGH, Gen. Mgr. *J. R. WOOD, Gen. Pass'r Agt.*

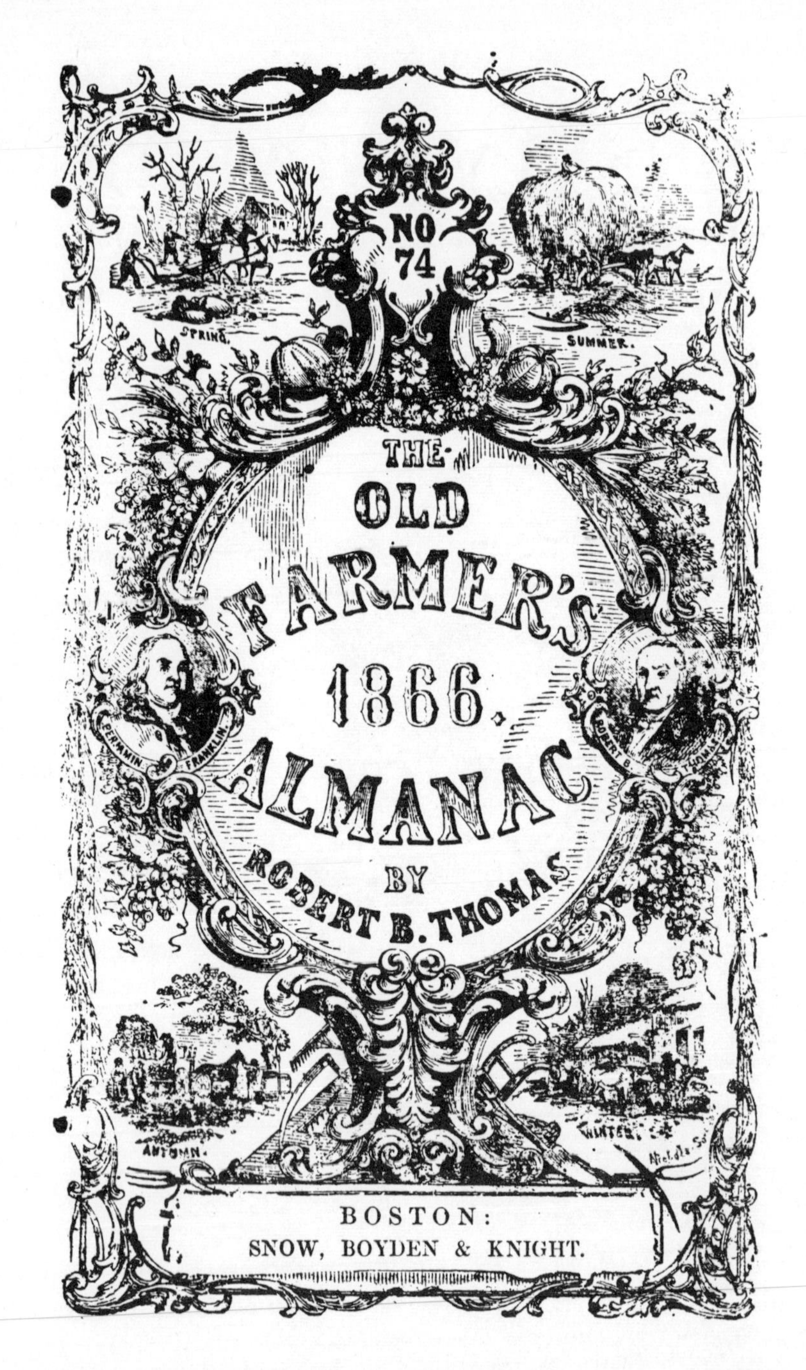

The Old Farmer's Almanac for 1866, "containing, besides the large number of Astronomical Calculations and the Farmer's Calendar for every month in the year, as great a variety as any other Almanack of new, useful, and entertaining matter."

XII

The Old Farmer *Grows Money, Too*

ONE OF THE refreshing facts about *The Old Farmer's Almanac* is that it looks about the same today as it did at the turn of the century. That is part of its charm. It is also a propitious sign that collecting almanacs can have its rewards because there are so many people interested in this form of paper antique. Yet most people who have not been bitten by the collecting bug would be astonished to learn how many hundreds of different almanacs were published and are still being published.

The almanac reached its peak as an advertising and merchandising tool during the late 1800's, especially during the reign of patent medicines. It was a natural for medicinal products such as kidney and liver cures, tonics, liniments, laxatives and blood purifiers. In the first place, the medicine men who toured the countryside dispensing their magical wares needed some substantial giveaway to attract crowds to their wagon or van. What better than an almanac, with a bright cover, useful purpose, and authoritative advice? Furthermore, almanacs could be produced inexpensively, easily packed in a small space, and were unbreakable and attractive to hand out—with appropriate flourishes and promises of priceless information within.

Some volumes were true almanacs, containing information about agriculture for the farmer, weather predictions, and data about the phases of the moon and changes in seasons. But all were alike in one way, whether they were valid compilations of factual material or simply catchalls of miscellaneous facts, jokes, puzzles, superstitions and sayings: They interspersed advertisements for the products manufactured by the publisher, and the best ones contained very subtle "advice" in the so-called editorial passages, which was designed to steer the reader toward the products advertised.

Collecting almanacs attracts people with a good sense of humor, for they find endless hours of enjoyment in perusing the pages of their acquisitions. A common section was one relating to the meaning of dreams, wherein you would find such morsels as these:

> *Abyss*: To dream of looking into one means that you will be confronted with threats of seizure to property.
> *Acid*: To drink any acid is an adverse dream, bringing you much anxiety.
> *Alligator*: To dream of an alligator, unless you kill it, is unfavorable to all persons connected with the dream.
> *Dentist*: You will have reason to doubt the sincerity of some person with whom you have dealings.
> *Dinner*: To dream that you ate dinner denotes that you will often have cause to think seriously of the necessities of life.
> *Jacket*: Wearing a small jacket indicates a small expedition; probably a picnic or informal party.
> *Kettle*: Scrubbing a kettle denotes an apology you will have to make for unkind words; if you are cooking something in one, an acquaintance will come to your door to make trouble.

Other popular sections which people expected to find dealt with horoscopes; signs of rain; fortune-telling by various

The Burdock Blood Bitter Almanac and *Key to Health,* 1885, published by Foster, Milburn & Co., Buffalo, New York. The last pages contained letters from grateful consumers attesting to the powers of the manufacturer's product.

means; the "Oraculum," or list of questions and answers about many things; fables, often with intricately interwoven advertising messages; puns and jokes; riddles and puzzles; and many others dealing with the interests of the era.

Some typical titles you will find for almanacs distributed by manufacturers of patent medicines are: *Rush's Almanac & Guide to Health, Swamp Root Dream Book Almanac, Warner's Safe-Cure Almanac, Dr. J. H. McLean's Family Almanac, The Ladies' Birthday Almanac* and *Dr. D. Jayne's Medical Almanac and Guide to Health.*

A common device in almanacs, attesting to the ingenuity of the authors, was the "ABC" format. This was usually a lengthy series of verses, each beginning with a letter of the alphabet and somehow managing to relate to the manufacturer's product. Characteristic is "ABC Jingles" (It is hardly necessary to mention the publisher!) from which come these samples:

A stands for all external Ails,
And Hanford's Balsam's many sales
Attest its use for Man or Beast
In the North or South, West or East. . . .

Q stands for Question; when you're sent
To buy a salve or liniment,
Be sure to ask in accents plain
For Hanford's Balsam, foe of pain. . . .

Z is where the alphabet ends;
We say goodbye to you, dear friends,
Recall the sayings you have passed—
Use Hanford's Balsam first and last.

Outside the medical field—by far the largest distributor of almanacs—there were hundreds of others published by the makers of all kinds of consumer products. And many almanacs were sold regionally by publishers, who made their profits not only on the cost charged to the buyer but on the sale of advertising space. Some examples of well-known regional almanacs are: *Hartford Almanac, New England Almanac, Tarrytown Almanac, Virginia Farmer's Almanac,* and *Hagerstown Town & Country Almanac.*

Others specialized in certain subject areas, such as the *Anti-Slavery Almanac* of the late 1830's, published in New England, and the *Presbyterian Almanac* of the 1840's.

If you study the categories of products that were in demand during the nineteenth century and at the beginning of the twentieth century, you will find that almost every one of them spawned almanacs and related publications. The A. L. Scovill

Company, for example, published *The Farmer & Mechanics Almanac* to promote its farm equipment. Presto Fertilizer Company in the later 1800's was a natural for an almanac to be distributed among its farm customers, not without numerous allusions to the advantages of its particular products. And you will find all kinds of almanacs, such as *The Life Boat,* published by the bottlers of sarsaparilla, one of the favorite drinks of the Victorian Age.

The origins of the modern almanac go well back into the eighteenth century, when the annual publication of each volume was a significant event in the life of Colonial America. Almost every household had need of the information contained in its pages in order to plan the planting of crops, care for the ill, educate the young, and take care of dozens of household chores. The pages also served as handy places, for those who could write, to jot down personal information, recipes, cures and agricultural data.

Forerunners of the almanac actually go back to about 1250 B.C., during the reign of Ramses II in Egypt, when a form of calendar was published with information about religious festivals, unlucky days, and predictions about the future for people born on certain days. The Greeks and Romans also used a form of almanac, and in the Middle Ages this kind of information was included in psalters, missals and other religious publications. In England, Roger Bacon is said to have been the first to use the word "almanack" in the recording of data about the movement of celestial bodies.

Collectors consider the late eighteenth century the period when the first so-called scientific almanacs appeared. These editions are rare, notably the *Nautical Almanac,* which began regular publication in London in 1767 and was the prototype for the much later *American Ephemeris and Nautical Almanac,* founded in 1855.

The most famous of all American editions and known to just about every schoolchild was Benjamin Franklin's creation, *Poor Richard's Almanack,* which was founded in 1732 and became a magnificent success. Franklin not only borrowed material from many of the English editions of the time, but developed his own particular style and themes. Chiefly, he attacked all the vices (laziness, avarice, thriftlessness, as well as the seven deadly sins) and exhorted the virtues (thrift, diligence, and early rising, to name a few). His brainchild was a bestseller for a quarter of a century. Needless to say, he has greatly enriched and enhanced the art of collecting. First editions are priceless, and every almanac collector of note would be happy to own an original Benjamin Franklin of any date.

The Old Farmer's Almanac is undoubtedly the most familiar one ever published. Started in 1793, by Robert Bailey Thomas, it has enjoyed almost one hundred and eighty years of continuous publication and is seen by hundreds of thousands of readers across the United States and Canada and in many countries abroad. One curious phenomenon is that its weather predictions, for an entire year ahead of time, are said to be about 80 percent accurate.

In general, almanacs have always owed their appeal to the innate desire of people to look into the future. In the early days, they catered to superstitions, myths and rituals. Later, around the beginning of the nineteenth century, they based as much of their information as possible on facts that could be wholly, or partially, documented, such as phases of the moon and the ebb and flow of the tides. Today they contain a combination of scientific information and mumbo jumbo, the latter usually presented in a spirit of fun or nostalgia.

As a collector, you will find few twentieth-century almanacs that are worth, monetarily, more than two or three dollars. And because so many millions of them have been published, many of the considerably older ones have a market value of only three or four dollars. Why do people collect these? For one thing, because they can occasionally increase the value by compiling specialized collections relating to certain products, industries or periods. In addition, they are interesting

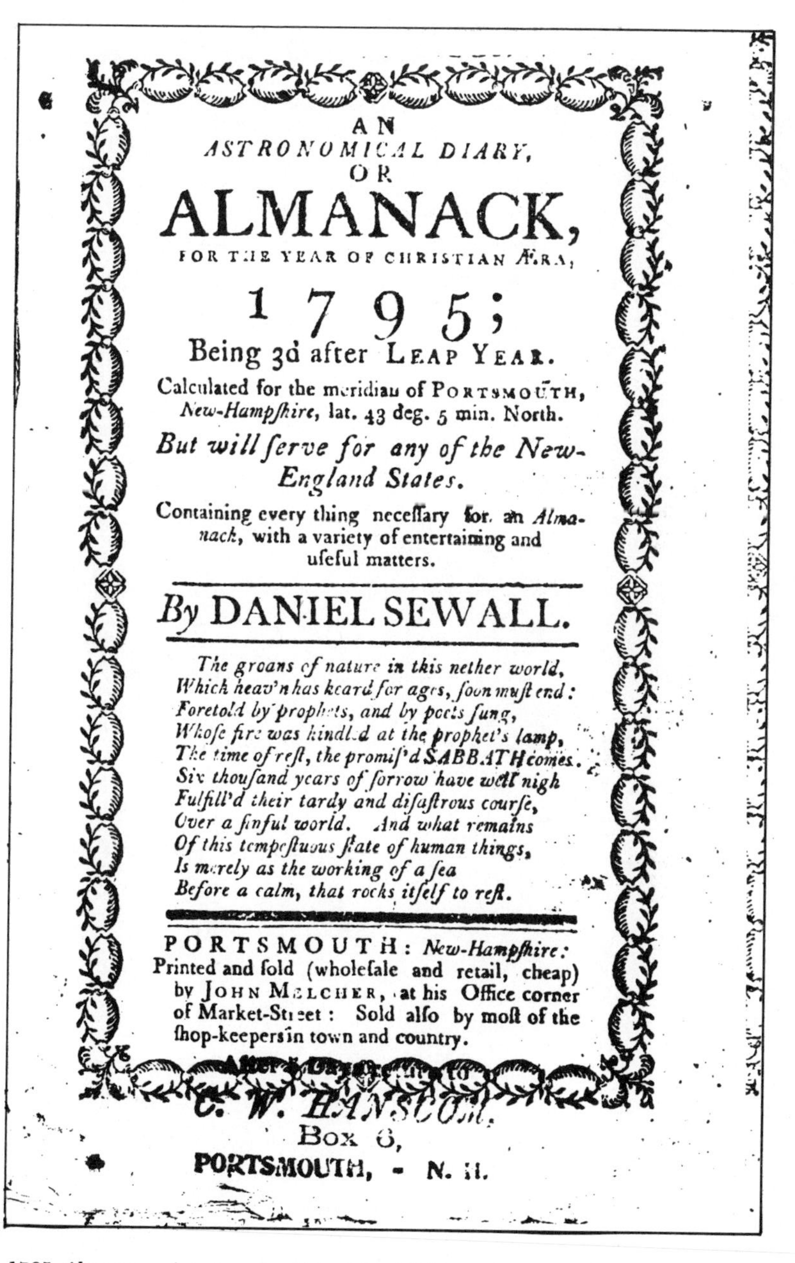

AN

ASTRONOMICAL DIARY,

OR

ALMANACK,

FOR THE YEAR OF CHRISTIAN ÆRA,

1795;

Being 3d after LEAP YEAR.

Calculated for the meridian of PORTSMOUTH, *New-Hampſhire*, lat. 43 deg. 5 min. North.

But will ſerve for any of the New-England States.

Containing every thing neceſſary for an *Almanack*, with a variety of entertaining and uſeful matters.

By DANIEL SEWALL.

The groans of nature in this nether world,
Which heav'n has heard for ages, ſoon muſt end:
Foretold by prophets, and by poets ſung,
Whoſe fire was kindled at the prophet's lamp,
The time of reſt, the promiſ'd SABBATH comes.
Six thouſand years of ſorrow have well nigh
Fulfill'd their tardy and diſaſtrous courſe,
Over a ſinful world. And what remains
Of this tempeſtuous ſtate of human things,
Is merely as the working of a ſea
Before a calm, that rocks itſelf to reſt.

PORTSMOUTH: *New-Hampſhire:*
Printed and ſold (wholeſale and retail, cheap) by JOHN MELCHER, at his Office corner of Market-Street: Sold alſo by moſt of the ſhop-keepers in town and country.

C. W. HANSCOM,
BOX 6,
PORTSMOUTH, - N. H.

1795 *Almanac* printed and sold by John Melcher, Portsmouth, New Hampshire. Measuring 6 1/2″ x 4″, it contained twenty-four pages.

historical records of America's past, despite the flights of fancy, outlandish glorification of certain nostrums, and weaknesses in factual research.

You will also find many of value—even great value—as you become more experienced in collecting. Following are some recent prices, showing a cross section of almanacs that you can easily acquire:

North American Almanac, 1776 . . . . $28
New England Almanac, 1783 . . . . $18
Hartford Almanac, 1796 . . . . $15
Hagerstown Town & Country Almanac, 1797
a first edition $50
Virginia Farmer's Almanac, 1808 . . . . $15
Ontario Almanac, 1828 . . . . $14
Life Boat (sarsaparilla) 1895 . . . . $8

As in the case of other paper acquisitions, the prices vary considerably depending on the condition of the almanac. Many have become yellowed or suffered fading of their colors. So if you are fortunate enough to locate finds that have been tucked away in albums or otherwise shielded from light, heat and other exposure, you may well discover that their values have proportionately increased.

XIII

Made to Order

FOR $14.95 YOU can buy a thick, large-page copy of an old-time mail-order catalogue. How old is it? Vintage 1880? 1900? 1915? Nothing of the sort. The volume referred to was published only a couple of years ago and is not an original at all, but a faithful reproduction.

Does this tell you anything? To the collector it is good news, for it means that there is tremendous interest in antique mail-order catalogues and that if a reproduction commands this price, the original might well be worth a great deal more, both financially and as a collector's exhibit. Of course, this is not always true, for some such publications that are truly antique from the standpoint of individual age are worth only two or three dollars on the open market and are not avidly sought. Yet it is a propitious sign.

Mail-order catalogues are fascinating to thumb through, to see what people wore, traveled in, played with, read, ate, drank, assuaged their ills with, or sent as gifts in generations past. That is why reproductions have sold in the millions and why you will find them in conspicuous places all over—on coffee tables, in offices, on library shelves, and in the waiting rooms of doctors and dentists. Nostalgia and curiosity motivate us, along with some uncontrollable masochistic urge to compare the unbelievably low prices of yesteryear with the escalating costs of products and services today.

As recently as the early 1960's, there was little interest in mail-order catalogues, whether original or reproduced. When found in attics, warehouses or other storage places, they were commonly destroyed or at the very most sold as scrap paper. And yet, as Carl W. Drepperd stated in *The Primer of American Antiques,* "Almost all that is known about pressed glass, Bennington pottery, weather vanes and similar objects derives from data and illustrations in trade catalogues." Recognizing this, certain historical societies and museums took steps to preserve these publications. Prized collections can be seen at institutions like New York's Metropolitan Museum of Art, the New York Historical Society, Harvard and a number of other universities. Yet even these centers became involved in amassing the publications more for a scholarly reason than for any other purpose.

You will find few product listings that predate the year 1800—if you do, snap them up if you possibly can. For some reason, the makers of buttons and clocks were the pioneers in this field, producing catalogues around 1790 and earlier. Oddly enough, there is no relationship between the two. Buttons were cheap, simple to describe, and very easy to depict in the simplest type of illustration, while clocks were expensive, complicated, and required the service of a good artist to render. One collector has suggested that clock catalogues came into being because their outer designs and inner works had to be sketched carefully before they could be made and craftsmen wanted the public to become aware of the wonders of their trade. Yet the same could be said of jewelry, fine glassware, musical instruments, or dozens of other products that required skill to design and produce.

It was not until the 1840's that manufacturers in many fields began publishing and distributing catalogues, mainly for the use of shopkeepers, who would order the merchandise. The

The styles and prices of 1933-34 shown in a page from the *Hollywood Style Edition* of the Chicago Mail Order Company catalogue. The cover displayed the insignia of a member of the NRA.

mail-order catalogue, printed in huge quantities and sent directly to prospective consumers, had little impact on merchandising in America until the latter part of the nineteenth century. Since it relied on postal services, it developed as the U.S. Post Office opened more and more branches and established clear postal rates.

Some collectors specialize in subject areas that are of particular interest to them. You can find marvelously detailed, illustrated catalogues for handguns, swords, farm equipment, tools, kitchen utensils, lamps, surgical instruments, barometers, navigational instruments and yachting supplies, automobile accessories, buggies, toys, seeds and plants, jewelry, silverware, butter molds, weather vanes, chairs, art prints, microscopes, gas engines, electric motors, fire-fighting equipment and engines, sewing machines, and—you name it.

The popularity (and value) of catalogues fluctuates to some extent with trends in antique collecting. If collectors suddenly start showing an interest in, say, cast-iron molds, paperweights or board games, you will find a consequent surge of interest in catalogues and other paper relating to those objects.

Catalogues that go back many years, and are most consistently of interest today, are those for general merchandise. This is the category, of course, in which you find the best sellers of Sears, Roebuck, Montgomery Ward, Wanamaker's, the early Macy's and other department stores. Very few of these that are in top condition and that go back beyond the early 1900's are easily attainable. Difficult to locate, too, are some of the pioneering advertising supplements with a catalogue format that were sandwiched between the pages of newspapers.

Some publications are classics of sheer amusement. Recalled with great joy and affection, for example, are the old Johnson & Smith catalogues, which listed everything imaginable to please and delight the most far-reaching desires of a schoolboy. They included outrageous practical jokes, such as fake sore thumbs, fake warts, exploding cigars, fart cushions, unlightable matches, viewers that blackened the victim's eye,

The cover of the first catalogue of products issued by the A. W. Chesterton Company in 1889, five years after the company's founding.

Courtesy, A. W. Chesterton Company

plate lifters, and dribble glasses. If you were inclined toward magic, you could order for anywhere from 10 cents to $1 such tricks as disappearing coins, marked cards, handkerchiefs that changed color, collapsible wands, invisible ink, boxes with secret compartments, and sprouting paper flowers. Some catalogues were far ahead of their time in offering ribald posters and provocative cartoons which, while they would hardly be second-glanced at today, were pretty bold for that era.

The early automobile catalogues have attracted large and

growing numbers of aficionados, their appeal and value strengthened by the fairly recent trend toward the restoration of antique cars. Such makes as Stutz, Nash, Duesenberg, Reo,Willys, Durant, Hupmobile, Stanley, Pierce-Arrow, Austin Benz, Daimler, Ford, Stearns, Napier, Vauxhall, and Mercedes are just a few of the magic words that make early car catalogues in great demand. Equally desired are maintenance and parts catalogues, some of which are of very practical value today in restoring and maintaining old cars. As is true with other types of catalogues, you can specialize in makes of cars, periods or geographical locations, and still never reach a saturation point.

Some collectors have found themselves drawn to the scientific catalogues, which are of more recent origin than most other types. Not too long ago, there were very few scientific supply houses specializing in sales to hospitals, schools, and industries. Today you will find a great proliferation of such publications. Many are extremely specialized, such as those which sell dimensional models and teaching aids to schools and colleges. Significantly, many of these catalogues that go back only fifteen or twenty years are greatly in demand. So if this particular subject interests you, now is a good time to buy these, since they are likely to be in mint condition and have a good chance of growing in value and interest in the not-too-distant future.

Before starting a collection of catalogues, consider the fact that they are, for the most part, bulky, take up a large amount of space, and are not always too easy to display. Unlike books, they tend to be floppy when placed on bookshelves, and they are not attractive when piled on top of each other. You should use protective covers as much as possible, especially for the older exhibits, since catalogues were usually printed on the cheapest paper that would suit the purpose, have lightweight jackets or covers, and are not always securely bound.

You will find a wide range of prices, of which the following are characteristic examples:

OUR 60-CENT PRINCESS HAIR RESTORER.

A WONDERFUL NEW HAIR TONIC AND PRODUCER.

No. 8N1101

Per Bottle, 60c.

PRINCESS HAIR RESTORER IS GOOD FOR BOTH MEN AND WOMEN, equally effective on men's, women's and children's hair.

Restores the Natural Color, Preserves and Strengthens the Hair for Years, Promotes the Growth, Arrests Falling Hair, Feeds and Nourishes the Roots, Cures Dandruff and Scurf, and Allays all Scalp Irritations.

Regular Retail Price, per bottle,	$1.00
Our Price, per bottle,	.60
Our Price, per dozen	6.00

Unmailable on account of weight.

The only absolutely effective, unfailingly successful, perfectly harmless, positively no-dye preparation on the market that restores gray hair to its natural and youthful color, removes crusts, scales and dandruff, soothes irritating, itching surfaces, stimulates the hair follicles, supplies the roots with energy and nourishment, renders the hair beautifully soft, and makes the hair grow WHEN ALL ELSE FAILS.

EVERY SINGLE BOTTLE OF PRINCESS HAIR RESTORER is compounded especially in our own laboratory by our own skilled chemists, and according to the prescription of one who has made the hair and scalp, its diseases and cure, a life study.

PRINCESS HAIR RESTORER IS NOT AN EXPERIMENT, not an untried unknown, quack remedy, depending on enormous, glittering advertisements for sales, but it is a preparation of the very finest and most expensive ingredients that will positively cure any case of falling hair, stimulate the growth of new hair on bald heads, cure dandruff and other diseases of the scalp.

ARE YOU BALD?
IS YOUR HAIR THIN OR FALLING OUT?
DOES YOUR HAIR COME OUT EASILY AND GATHER ON THE COMB AND BRUSH WHEN YOU BRUSH IT?
DOES YOUR HEAD ITCH?
DO YOU HAVE DANDRUFF OR SCURF AND DO WHITE, DUST-LIKE PARTICLES SETTLE ON YOUR COAT COLLAR?
IS YOUR HAIR STIFF AND COARSE AND HARD TO BRUSH?
IS YOUR HAIR FADING OR HAS IT TURNED PREMATURELY GRAY?

IF YOUR HAIR SUFFERS in any one or more of these particulars, we would urge you by all means to order a bottle of **Princess Hair Restorer** as a trial, for speedy relief. Use it according to directions and you will be surprised and delighted at the wonderful results. **PRINCESS HAIR RESTORER NEVER FAILS.** It acts direct on the tiny roots of the hair, giving them required fresh nourishment, starts quick and energetic circulation in every hair cell, tones up the scalp, freshens the pores, stops falling and sickly hair, changes thin hair to a fine heavy growth, puts new life in dormant, sluggish hair cells on bald heads, producing in a short time an **absolutely new growth of hair. If your hair is fading or turning gray,** one bottle of Princess Hair Restorer will give it healthy life, renew its original color and restore it to youthful profusion and beauty.

USE IT ALWAYS IF YOU WANT A HEAD OF FINE, SILKY, GLOSSY HAIR, THE PRIDE OF EVERY WOMAN.

Princess Hair Restorer Grows Hair Like This

AS A CURE FOR DANDRUFF, as a tonic for thin and scanty hair, Princess Hair Restorer acts with quick and wonderful success. It removes crusts and scales, keeps the scalp clean and healthy, the roots at once respond to its vigorous action, dandruff is banished and a thick and healthy growth of hair is assured.

FOR A TOILET ARTICLE, as a fine hair dressing, no one who takes any pride in a nice head of hair can afford to be without a bottle always on the dresser. **Princess Hair Restorer** is delicately perfumed, and one light application imparts a delightful, refined fragrance. Neither oils, pomades, vaseline or other greases are required with our preparation.

DON'T SEND AWAY TO SOME UNKNOWN CONCERN for a so-called **Hair Grower**, that promises everything in their advertisement and do no good whatever, and may do a great deal of harm. **Don't send away to a cheap specialist and pay $1.00, $1.50 or $2.00 a bottle** for a worthless and perhaps injurious preparation. Don't be misled by catchy advertisements with baits of free trial sample bottle and fake examination—such people will draw you in, make you believe something awful is the matter and scare you into paying enormous prices for alleged remedies, when you get the **genuine, tried, tested, proven and guaranteed Princess Hair Restorer at 60 cents a bottle,** the actual cost of the ingredients and labor of bottling, with our one small profit added.

PRINCESS HAIR RESTORER IS ABSOLUTELY HARMLESS. IT IS NOT A DYE. It will not injure the most delicate hair, it will not stain the daintiest head dress. Princess Hair Restorer works wonders with the hair. We get letters daily from people telling how much good it has done for them. It will do the same for you. You can sell a dozen bottles at a profit to yourself in your immediate neighborhood to people who see the good it has done and the wonderful results on your hair. **Order a bottle at 60 cents, which you can easily sell at $1.00 each,** and if you do not find it all and more than we claim for it, if you do not find it is just the hair tonic you want, stimulating the growth, cleansing the scalp, stopping hair from falling out, restoring natural color, curing dandruff or promoting a new growth of hair on a bald head, return it to us at once **AND WE WILL CHEERFULLY REFUND YOUR MONEY.**

OUR WHITE LILY FACE WASH, 40 CENTS PER BOTTLE.

THE LADIES' FAVORITE TOILET PREPARATION.

An Invaluable Remedy for Pimples, Freckles, Sallowness, Roughness, Wrinkles, Tan, Blackheads and all Irritations and Imperfections of the Skin.

Retail Price	$0.75
Our Price	.40
Our Price per doz.	$4.20

THE FAMOUS WHITE LILY FACE WASH FOR BEAUTIFYING THE COMPLEXION SOLE AGENTS SEARS, ROEBUCK & CO CHEAPEST SUPPLY HOUSE ON EARTH CHICAGO ILL.

No. 8N1104

Recommended by Thousands of Beautiful Women.

DIFFERENT FROM MOST COMPLEXION PREPARATIONS, our White Lily Face Wash contains not a particle of lead, silver, sulphur, arsenic, mercury or other poisonous mineral by which most complexion remedies, and particularly the advertised ones, produce a temporary smoothness and brilliancy of the skin. **White Lily Face Wash is clear and harmless as water,** contains no poison, no sediment, nothing to hurt the most tender and delicate skin. Its effect in quickly removing pimples, blackheads, freckles, roughness and tan is simply wonderful. **White Lily Face Wash smoothes out wrinkles and roughness,** all imperfections and irritations of the skin disappear, restores the delicate tint of girlhood and youth, leaving the skin soft and velvety. **Nothing is more attractive than a lovely complexion.**

DO YOU WANT TO BE BEAUTIFUL? Do you want a spotless skin, a matchless complexion, the envy and pride of every one? **Send for a bottle of White Lily Face Wash,** use it according to directions and a perfect complexion will be the result. **We positively guarantee White Lily Face Wash** to permanently cure pimples, blackheads and other eruptions of the skin, to completely remove tan, freckles, blotches, sallowness, roughness, flabbiness, wrinkles and all other imperfections of the skin, face, neck, bust, arms and hands.

WHITE LILY FACE WASH has a wonderful sale. The market is full of injurious complexion preparations. Many, in fact, most of these preparations contain lead, arsenic, bismuth or mercury and are really dangerous in their effects. **You can protect yourself** from serious skin diseases by using our **White Lily Face Wash. Take no chances. Avoid all danger.** Use only a preparation that is absolutely harmless, one that you can depend on for a spotless skin, a positive beautifier that has been recommended by thousands of ladies.

USE ONLY THE GENUINE WHITE LILY FACE WASH, PREPARED AND SOLD BY US.

104 Regular retail price per bottle, 75c; our price, per dozen, $4.20; each ....(If by mail, postage and tube extra, 18 cents) 40c

A page from a special drug catalogue issued by Sears, Roebuck & Company advertises Princess Hair Tonic Restorer and "Our White Lily Face Wash, the Ladies' Favorite Toilet Preparation."

Montgomery Ward Catalogues

1930 .... $3

1931 .... $18

1921 .... $30

1920 .... $35

Sears, Roebuck Catalogues

1952 .... $5

1931 .... $15

1926 .... $30

1922 .... $35

Sommers & Company, 1908 .... $17.50

Lippincott, soda water dispensers,
fountain equipment, 1883 .... $16

Pratt & Whitney, milling machines
and dies, 1908 .... $15

Hirshberg Art Co., 1903 .... $17

Benj. Allen & Co., jewelry, 1900 .... $30

Burr Stone Mills & Mill Machinery,
mills, separators, etc., 1886 .... $50

Macy's, New York City, 1905 .... $50

Goodell-Pratt, tools, 1926 . . . . $25

Akron Cultivator Co., 1895 . . . . $8.50

Jordan-Marsh & Co., 1885 . . . . $30

Lyon, Healy Co., musical instruments
and supplies, 1912 . . . . $25

Wanamaker's, 1903 . . . . $7.50

Among some of the most desirable and most expensive of the older catalogues are a 1902 Montgomery Ward valued at $100; a 1904 Sears, Roebuck at $95; and an Ames Sword Co., of Chicopee, Massachusetts, 1890, at more than $100 in mint condition. As you can see, the value often depends just as much on the subject as on the age.

XIV

It's Your Turn to Bid

A COLLECTOR OF paper antiques in Wisconsin is an avid, almost obsessive, bridge player. If he cannot find a good game going, with experienced partners, he will talk almost *anyone* into playing. He has played cards not only in homes and clubs, but on commuting trains, on boats, on planes, in men's locker rooms, on the beach, on picnics and at least once on a raft anchored off a friend's dock on a lake.

As though this were not enough, he also collects playing cards. And he collects somewhat the way he plays, trying to use the strength of one suit to win points in all the others. He has a positive genius for picking up a deck of ancient playing cards at an auction or sale, selling it, and then buying three or four old packs with the money. Since many of the latter turn out to be almost as valuable as the original and can also be used for trading purposes, he keeps building his collection without ever seeming to spend any money— a fine trick if you can swing it.

Most players spend little time contemplating the design of the cards they are using, other than remarking on occasion that a certain deck is "pretty" or "unusual" or seems to shuffle easily. Yet playing cards have a very long history and are highly prized as collector's items by thousands of people. Since playing cards were used hundreds of years ago in Europe and long before that in the Orient, collectors can acquire anything from recent novelties to very rare, even priceless, antiques.

In *The Complete Book of Collecting Hobbies*, William Paul Bricker attributes the origin of playing cards to an anonymous gamesman in China during the reign of Suen-Ho, A.D. 1120. As the story goes, he was a nobleman with a harem on his hands. And as he grew older and less interested in the ladies, he devised a crude form of playing cards to keep them amused and leave him to other pursuits. Whether or not this is true, the playing card as we know it had its origins in Europe in the fourteenth century. A manuscript in the British Museum depicts a card game in progress, with three players. The design arrangements on these cards are not unlike what we see today.

Records show that during the fifteenth century, playing cards were being made in quantity, printed and hand-colored, in Germany, Italy and England. The earliest suits were made up of combinations of hearts, bells, leaves, swords, batons, cups, leaves and units of money. The present-day assemblage of spades, hearts, diamonds and clubs was adopted in France during the sixteenth century. At first, the full deck consisted of seventy-eight cards but was later changed to the fifty-two that have become standard.

You will note that the earlier playing cards did not have any decorative backs. At first they were plain. Then, in the early 1800's, the French began using a colored marbled design on the back. The Germans followed suit, while the Italians began experimenting with designs cut from wood blocks. It was not until the latter part of the nineteenth century that cards were designed with illustrations. In England it became popular for manufacturers to imprint pictures of members of the royal family.

In America during the early part of the nineteenth century, the best cards often had portraits of George Washington, John Adams and other Presidents and statesmen in the medallion style of the day. As one collector pointed out, "Playing cards were sometimes used for political and propaganda purposes, to promote the causes that the owners espoused." Thus you will find cards, though rare, which carried the portraits or campaign symbols and slogans of candidates running for office. During the Civil War, it became popular to display and use cards bearing the flags of the North and the South or of generals and admirals who had achieved recent notoriety.

There was a period when the kings and queens on the counting side of the cards were depicted as heroes and heroines of the day. One famous deck shows Victor Hugo as the king of hearts. But, gradually, designers began to standardize the images. The cards we play with today— and which have been around for decades— depict Charlemagne (742-814) as the king of hearts in a manner that suggests the art style of the fifteenth century. The queen of hearts is said to be Judith of Bavaria, Charlemagne's daughter-in-law, while the queen of spades is Pallas Athena, the goddess of war and of wisdom.

Attempts were made for many generations to standardize cards in other ways. Yet this did not really come about until the latter part of the nineteenth century. The date 1877 is significant in one way. Before that date there were no index numbers in the corner, and after that date there were.

Inventors and designers have come up with just about every conceivable shape that could still be shuffled and held in the hand and sorted. Some collectors delight in collecting the most bizarre cards they can find— triangular, oval, round, diamond-shaped, as well as square, and the now standard oblong shape. You will find that the older packs are about one-quarter or even one-half inch wider than present-day cards. It is said that the present width, 2 1/4 inches, was accepted as standard when bridge took over from whist in popularity around the 1880's. Holding thirteen cards at one time was difficult with the wider pack.

No one knows exactly who first discovered the value of the playing card for advertising and promotional purposes. It is known that there were a few such cards around the middle of the last century. But the real influx of advertising cards came in the early 1880's, beginning largely with steamship, railroad and other transportation companies whose services had pictorial interest and could easily be portrayed on the backs of cards. One of the largest groups of collectors restrict themselves just to advertising types. From the middle of the 1880's right on up until today, the use of cards for advertising, promotion and publicity has become widespread. Advertisers tried all kinds of experiments, sometimes changing the traditional spades, hearts, diamonds and clubs to products which they distributed, such as bottled drinks, hardware or medicines. The most common and successful, from the advertising standpoint, that is, were ones that reproduced appealing art.

The most valuable cards to collect and the most difficult to locate are those that represent different periods or styles. These have considerable historical interest, and many are so rare that they are seldom found outside museum exhibits. If you can locate any examples that predate about 1820, you will be fortunate indeed.

Another reason for the rarity of playing cards is that they have always been considered expendable. Throughout the ages, good cardplayers have always thrown cards away once they showed any signs of wear that might give opponents clues as to the suit and denomination. For this reason, too, the condition of a pack that is difficult to find can be a key factor in the value and selling cost. A set of boxed playing cards with a local scene from New England might be worth $5 if used, and twice that if in mint condition, since cards of this type are relatively easy to find and were more often preserved as souvenirs than they were used for playing.

Some people collect only jokers, since, no matter how badly a pack may have been mangled through constant use, these cards are generally set aside. Also, this type of collection is much easier to store and display. But jokers alone or any other individual cards do not have the value of a full deck unless they happen to be from a rare pack.

If you travel a great deal, you will notice that certain countries and regions tend to have cards with designs patterned after ones that originated there many years ago. So if you cannot locate old decks, you can at least acquire ones that are typical of the location.

How and where do you collect playing cards? You will rarely find them offered on the open market. Skimming through offerings by traders and dealers, you will see thirty or forty listings of posters, mail-order catalogues, comic books or postcards, for example, for every lone offer of a pack of playing cards. So if you have a chance to buy duplicate sets, by all means do so. You can then use them for trading with other collectors. Secondhand shops and junk shops will occasionally have playing cards for sale, and you can usually locate a deck or two at an auction of contents from a private home. If you have a chance prior to the auction, look through bureaus, desks and other furniture with drawers to see whether any cards have, by chance, been left in them. Antique dealers occasionally come by old cards this way and will sell them at reasonable cost, since they are not in their usual line of items.

Some of the really old and historic packs are very valuable antiques in their own right. Rare Italian cards from the sixteenth century, for instance, are worth $600 or more. Others from the seventeenth and eighteenth centuries may sell for anywhere from $150 to $500 a pack.

Do not overlook friends and relatives as sources of cards. In fact, if people know that you collect them, they will usually be delighted to look for acquisitions for you— while looking in old family trunks and other storage places, while foraging around in secondhand shops, or when traveling abroad.

One of the best pieces of advice for an amateur collector— of just about anything— is to talk enthusiastically about your hobby and show people what you are collecting, on every possible occasion. You will be surprised at what turns up via friends, relatives, business colleagues, acquaintances in organizations, neighbors and others.

XV

Sharps and Flats

"Old Hymn Is New Hit in Europe."

"AFTER RESTING MODESTLY for almost 200 years in English hymnals," began an account in the New York *Times* of April 15, 1972, "the ode, 'Amazing Grace' by the London divine, John Newton, became a hit song in Europe this week, topping popularity charts in Britain and on the Continent."

To collectors of antique sheet music and especially to any who happened to possess one of the earliest printed versions of the hymn, this announcement was indeed good news. For it is just this kind of incident that can spark further interest in paper antiquing in general and perhaps bring about an increase in demand and value for the particular item receiving publicity.

If you are a music lover and have an urge to take up collecting as a hobby, there can be no more natural and satisfying field than sheet music. Even if you know little about music, play no instrument, and have a tin ear, you might well find yourself fascinated by a number of appeals, including the historical significance, the range of subjects, humorous verses (often not intentional), imaginative designs, themes, and the nostalgia of it all.

The origins of sheet music lie in the old hymnals, as in the case of "Amazing Grace," and in other religious publications of great historical worth, such as the *Bay Psalm Book*, published in Massachusetts by the Puritans and based on an earlier English psalter. But as new printing processes were perfected and as the piano became the main attraction in the typical American parlor, publishers saw a gold mine in selling individual sheets of music, which they could promote and peddle all over the country by the thousands.

In America, the first songs to become popular, back in the seventeenth century, were religious in nature. But as the country began to emerge politically, numerous political songs evolved. One such was the "Liberty Song," first published in a Boston newspaper in 1768. It entreated people to band against the "tyrannous" Townshend Acts of 1767, which were examples of taxation without representation. Early songs of this type are of great value to collectors.

Another, and probably the most popular of all songs of the Revolutionary period, was "Chester," which bravely proclaimed that the singers trusted in God and did not fear the tyrants who shook their iron rods or the slave traders with their chains. "Yankee Doodle," which is much more familiar, was another that long endured. Collectors look for a few dozen others from this era, including "Revolutionary Tea," "Johnny Has Gone for a Soldier," and "Hail Columbia," which played up the glories of the United States in 1798, when the fledgling country was on the brink of war with France.

After the War of 1812, the political, nationalistic themes gave way to a much more casual and romantic outlook, as bands of adventurers headed westward across the prairies and mountains and along the waterways through the wilderness. This period gave birth to many frontier songs which were sung by the pioneers, often while they were working or traveling across the country. The popularity of these songs and lyrics reached a peak in the late 1840's and 1850's. "Song of the Kansas Emigrant," with words by the famous John Greenleaf Whittier, is a characteristic example.

Another, familiar to almost everyone, was "Shanadoah" (often misspelled "Shenandoah," the spelling most common today). It was named for an Indian chief who had a daughter of great beauty and was sung initially by riverboatmen and sailors at sea, who pictured themselves in love with Shanadoah's beautiful daughter. The lilt of the rolling waters and the romantic longing for the Indian maiden are dreams as familiar today as they were more than one hundred years ago. Collectors pine for early versions of this, along with such other delights as "Tommy's Gone to Hilo," "Hey, Betty Martin!" and those two most rustic of rustic tunes, "The Farmer in the Dell" and "Pop! Goes the Weasel."

It was during this period, too, that love songs and folk songs captured the American fancy. Some of the most notable were "Greenfields," based on a hymn, "From Greenland's Icy Mountains," which in 1824 was one of the first examples of popular music in single-sheet form, "Down Came an Angel," and "I Wonder When I Shall Be Married."

But for many collectors few categories have as much appeal as the songs of the early minstrel stage in the United States, among them such notable pieces as Stephen Foster's "My Old Kentucky Home," a plantation melody first published in 1852; "Camptown Races," which Foster composed as a blend of several black spirituals of the day; and his "Oh! Susanna," which he wrote and sold to a Cincinnati music publisher for one hundred dollars when he was only twenty-two. Although Foster did not see any share of the great profits derived by the publisher, especially when it became the "unofficial anthem" of the forty-niners on their way to California, it was instrumental in launching him in his famous career.

Other collector's items of the minstrel period include "Old Dan Tucker," "Angelina Baker," "Old Zip Coon," "Lubly Fan, Will You Come Out Tonight?" and "The Old Gray Goose."

It could be said that sheet music really came into its own in the middle of the nineteenth century, when the family piano was as much the center of attention across America as the television set is today. To meet the increasing demands for family harmonizing, sheet music came strongly into the picture, published in great quantities and distributed everywhere, from the largest cities to the smallest towns. A collection of such music provides an extraordinary image of the social history of the country, not only in the changing tastes in music, but in the illustrations. It became popular for publishers to decorate the covers with fancy artwork, much of it rivaling only the lyrics in sentimentality.

You will find an enduring record of the famous entertainers of each era, along with military scenes, animals and birds, mountains, forests, lakes and other scenery, and a wide variety of musical instruments. European publishers tended to go in for more elaborate artwork and fancier decoration than did their American counterparts. Certain names became associated with different forms of music, such as John Brandard, who specialized in opera and ballet, and Alexander Laby, whose fields were ballads and religious themes.

During the heyday of the parlor piano, many songs were naturally composed to reflect the joys of the home and the family. Probably the most famous and certainly the most familiar was "Home, Sweet Home," with words by John Howard Payne and music by Sir Henry Rowley Bishop. Ironically, Payne was an actor who traveled from place to place so regularly that he never did get around to owning a home. The ballad, composed in 1823, was first sung in England in a musical, *Clari, or the Maid of Milan.* It was made popular by the lovely Jenny Lind, "The Swedish Nightingale," who is said to have sung it at that most famous of all American homes, the White House.

Other songs of that period were "Woodman, Spare That Tree," perhaps one of the first environmental pleas on record; "Columbia, the Gem of the Ocean," reflecting the pride of the American people in the country, which was rapidly expanding and assuming its place in the world of nations; and "Tippecanoe and Tyler, Too," a forerunner of many later political songs and written to promote the campaign of William Henry Harrison for President of the United States in 1840. The name refers to a battle in 1811 on the banks of the Tippecanoe River

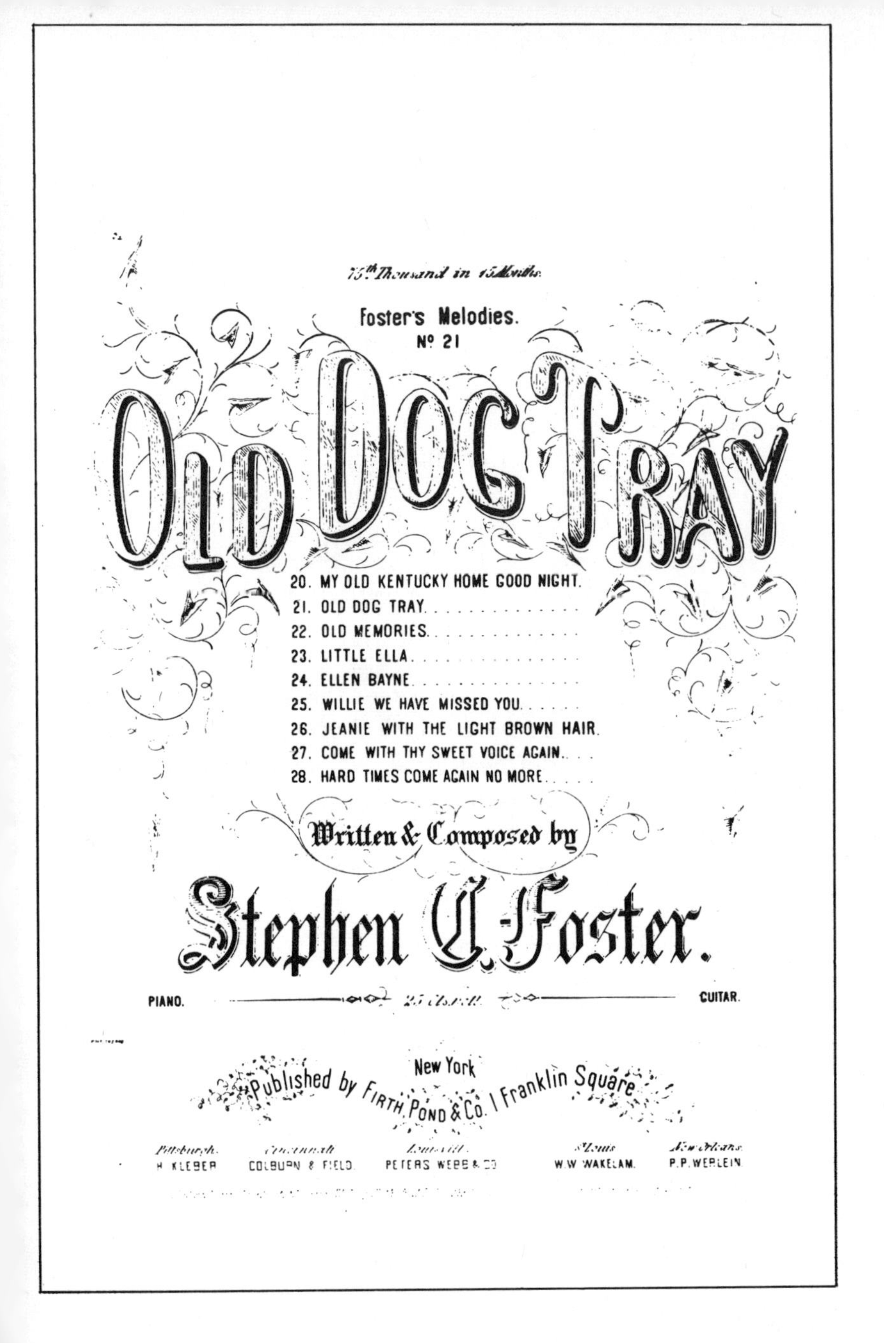

itle page of the sheet music for Stephen Foster's "Old Dog Tray," copyrighted in 1853.

in Indiana, in which forces under Harrison fought the Indians.

As everyone knows, the Civil War was an enormous inspirational force when it came to composing songs and writing lyrics. At the time the war began, American song writing was at a dismal ebb, and in fact, many of the songs of the pre-Civil War period were sickly sentimental, dreary and repetitive. However, that does not mean that such songs have lost favor as collector's items. Many collectors, in fact, find it amusing to acquire such works that are dripping with oversentimentality and often illustrated with romantic scenes that provoke chuckles today.

But with the coming of the tragic War Between the States, composers found fresh, exciting opportunities to create works that were sometimes to affect the very course of battle. In this category are such stirring numbers as "The Battle Hymn of the Republic," an old tune given immortal words by Julia Ward Howe and which served as one of the North's greatest inspirations. Her version was published in what is a desirable collector's item, the February, 1862, issue of *Atlantic Monthly.*

Described as one of "the most hateful songs" written during the Civil War was "Marching Through Georgia," commemorating the devastating march of General William Tecumseh Sherman through the state in 1864. This is a good example of one type of song that particularly interests collectors because it has had many later adaptations, the first editions of which can add to the value and interest of a collection. "Marching," for instance, was adapted as inspiration for British troops in India as a tune of conquest by the Japanese when they were invading Manchuria; and later to strengthen the morale of American troops in World War II, particularly during campaigns in the desert of North Africa.

In addition to the strongly inspirational songs, the Civil War gave us some very tender pieces that have endured through succeeding generations, such as "When Johnny Comes Marching Home." For perhaps the first time, Europe began to recognize that the United States had a vibrant, forceful musical culture and strong creativity.

"Yes, I Would the War Were Over," sheet music published in the July, 1863, issue of *Peterson's Magazine*.

Not recognized at the time—and indeed not for many years—was the vitality of the music of the American black, a musical tradition that dated from the early days of slavery in the New World. But it was the Civil War and the period just following that brought this music to public attention. Very few of the evolving spirituals achieved publication until the 1860's, a period that is significant among collectors of such pieces. The first authentic collection of black music in the United States was *Slave Songs of the United States*, published in 1867. "Nobody Knows De Trouble I've Had" typifies this form of music. Collectors prize early publishings of these and other spirituals, such as the very moving "Deep River," "Swing Low, Sweet Chariot," and that lively number, "When the Saints Go Marching In."

It was not long after sheet music became popular that manufacturers began to see its value for advertising and promotion. Some popular nineteenth-century forerunners of radio and TV commercials were "The Sewing Machine Polka," to extol the pleasures of machines made by the firm of Wheeler

& Wilson; "The Black Cook," for Charter Oak Ranges; and "Good Old Sweet Ham," composed, written and published by the Magnolia Ham Company.

Each new era in American history brought with it memorable songs that characterized the people, the political and economic climate, and the events of the day. As America expanded in the latter part of the nineteenth century, the music related to transportation ("The Wabash Cannon Ball"), folk heroes and villains ("Jesse James"), religion ("Old-Time Religion"), agriculture ("Bringing in the Sheaves"), immigrants from abroad ("I'll Take You Home Again, Kathleen"), and other topics uppermost in people's minds.

The coming of the automobile was reflected in songs like "In My Merry Oldsmobile" and the appeal of the rapidly growing cities in pieces like "The Sidewalks of New York," which would later be revived as an effective political campaign theme. Nostalgia had its place in "Sweet Adeline" and patriotism in "America the Beautiful." World War I had its famous "Over There," "Pack Up Your Troubles in Your Old Kit Bag" and "Keep the Home Fires Burning."

Prices for sheet music and other forms in which songs were published vary tremendously. For two or three dollars, you can pick up song sheets for "I'm Forever Blowing Bubbles," "The Man I Love," "I Cried for You" and "I Wonder What's Become of Sally." You will pay a little more for "The Sheik of Araby," "A Pretty Girl Is Like a Melody," "Toot Toot Tootsie, Goodbye" and "Way Down Yonder in New Orleans."

Copies of the earliest sheet music in top condition are not easy to come by, and many are worth $30, $50 and more than $100. Right now, song sheets from World War I are highly prized by many collectors. While some are relatively cheap—about four or five dollars for "Pack Up Your Troubles" or "There's a Long, Long Trail Awinding," for example—a few are quite high. A 1918 copy of "Over There," with an illustration of soldiers by Norman Rockwell, fetches $25. Other editions of the same song, though, can be bought for about $10 to $15.

XVI

Ten Thrills per Page

> The blood dripping down over his eyes almost blinded Scott. He could hardly breathe in the cloud of smoke from his crippled engine that enveloped the cockpit of his Spad. Yet he was determined, with sure death staring him in the face, that he would take the Green Baron, Manfred von Murgenthaller, down in flames with him. He wiped the blood from his eyes long enough to spot the green tail of the Baron's Fokker ahead in his gun sights. With his bullet-punctured left hand, he squeezed off the final remaining burst of incendiaries from his Vickers. Tat-tat-tat-tat. Now there was a speck of red on that hated green of the enemy's tail section. The Baron was going to go down in flames! Scott slumped back in his cockpit, fighting to remain conscious. . . .

SO RUNS A typical passage from one of the pulp magazines of the 1920's devoted to World War I aces and aerial battles. If you decide to collect in this medium and specialize in subject areas that interest you, collecting old pulp magazines and dime novels can be exuberant good fun, as well as rewarding in other ways.

A word of caution for the beginner (and sometimes the more experienced hand as well): There are so many, many different collectible magazines and books that it is better to aim at

The logo for *The Judge,* a weekly magazine of political commentary and satire. The October 28, 1882, issue contained "judgments" on Henry Ward Beecher, Victor Hugo and Grover Cleveland, among others. Political memorabilia could be the basis for a handsome and valuable collection of paper antiques.

certain categories than to acquire indiscriminately. What appeals to you—history, motion pictures, nature, personalities, Western lore, humor, exploration, adventure, the sea, family life, science, or any of hundreds of other subjects?

People who collect right across the board, regardless of topic, generally confine themselves to a particular era. This may be defined by historical events, politics or sociological trends. Some further limit themselves geographically or ethnically, or both. Values play a part, too, in determining how, why and what to collect. For example, it is well known that *complete* sets of magazines are often treasured—such as *National Geographic, St. Nicholas Magazine, Puck, Judge* and *Harper's.*

With newspapers, you have to be much more selective to avoid enormous and unwieldy collections. Some people collect the very first issues—Volume I, Number 1—of all kinds of newspapers. Others stick to the historical period when papers were few in number, from the end of the seventeenth century to the beginning of the nineteenth. Often the headlines help determine the value. Good examples are some displayed at the Overseas Press Club in New York City announcing momentous events as the destruction of the battleship *Maine,* the bombing of Pearl Harbor, and the assassination of President John F. Kennedy.

Interest in magazine topics is an ever-changing

TELEGRAPH TO THE HERALD.

FROM

WASHINGTON.

ALL QUIET AT HARPER'S FERRY.

STRENGTH OF THE REBEL ARMY

GEN. HUNTER RECOVERING FROM HIS WOUNDS.

REPORT OF THE POTTER EXAMINING COMMITTEE.

162 Disloyal Clerks Reported

—TO THE—

HEADS OF DEPARTMENTS!

NOT ONE DISAFFECTED ARMY OFFICER!

The London Times Correspondent REFUSED A PASS TO CROSS THE POTOMAC!

Announcement of the engagement at Harper's Ferry appeared in the morning edition of the Boston *Herald* on August 23, 1861.

phenomenon, much like the trends in fashions. A few years ago, no one had much interest in the old movie magazines. We were still too close to the movies as a common form of current entertainment, without much thought about the past. But with the coming of television an interesting change took place. TV stations began keeping on hand small stocks of movies, which they could throw into the breach whenever shows were postponed or canceled. Because cost was an important factor, they often used movies that were fairly old for which there were only modest rerun fees.

Oddly enough, certain fans began taking an interest in the oldies. Today there is a revival of pictures from the World War I era and before as well as later productions that starred Charlie Chaplin, W. C. Fields and Harold Lloyd. Paralleling this has been an equal interest among collectors of publications in the old movie magazines, like *Screenland,* first published in 1920, and *Photoplay,* first published in 1911.

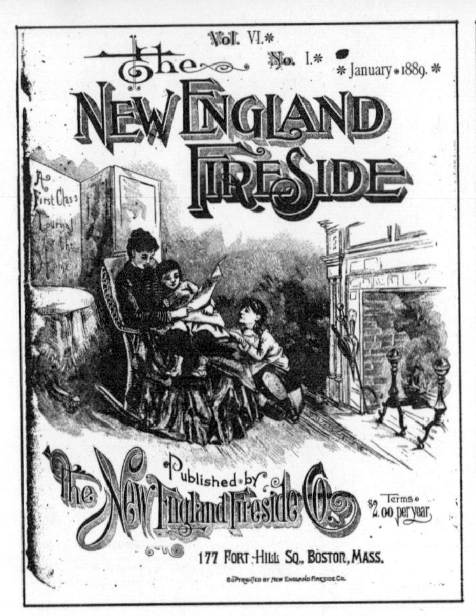

Covers from *The New England Fireside* and *Wood's Household Magazine.* The March, 1873, issue of *Wood's,* shown here, contained an article by Harriet Beecher Stowe and pieces on Elizabeth Blackwell and "The Use of the Corset."

There are other categories which remain fairly stable, attracting their particular devotees. These include the World War I air magazines, the Westerns, the mystery publications and the true-confession types. Humor magazines, like *Judge,* the original *Life* and *Punch,* have a steady demand. For some reason, possibly because of the sharp political satire, copies of *Judge* are more than 200 percent higher than they were a few years ago.

Many people, especially those who live in apartments or small homes, where there is a limited amount of space, collect covers only. They sometimes mount these on cardboard—samples of the old *Saturday Evening Post, Leslie's Weekly, Scribner's Monthly, Century Illustrated Monthly Magazine, Peterson's Magazine, New England Fireside, Household* and others—thus compiling a graphic history of Americana. One of the biggest drawbacks to this approach is that the collectors miss the fun of having the contents to read or the old advertisements to peruse. And there is a danger in ripping off covers and tossing the rest of the magazine away. Even though a particular magazine may have little monetary value when

A COLORED FASHION PLATE IN THIS NUMBER!!

MAY.

Cover of *Godey's Lady's Book,* 1853. Subscriptions were "$3 per annum, in advance." Issues of *Godey's,* particularly those containing color plates, are many times more valuable today.

acquired, its price can skyrocket rather suddenly— but only for the whole magazine, in good condition, and not the cover alone.

Values may rise because of the contents, the authors or the artists. If you find a magazine with an early cover by Maxfield Parrish, Howard Chandler Christy or Rockwell Kent, the cover could have considerable worth. However, if work by the artist is included *inside*, then the value would go up far more for the undamaged issue *in toto*. Fashions may play their part, too. Copies of *Godey's Lady's Book* and *Peterson's Magazine,* which sold for $10 to $15 a few years ago, range in price from about $30 upward. Why? There is no scientific, or even logical, reason, just a new interest in fashions and trends.

Rarity plays a substantial part in the desirability of certain publications, too. In the mid-sixties, you could buy a set of the old *St. Nicholas Magazine*, from its first issue to 1900, for about $25. Now this magazine seems almost nonexistent, at least on the open market, and it is anyone's guess as to what a complete set, in top condition, would be worth. Color also carries some weight, particularly in publications that ran color plates and inserts suitable for framing or mounting in scrapbooks.

Children's magazines form a completely different and easily defined category which has great appeal to thousands of collectors. *St. Nicholas Magazine*, which was founded in 1873 and ran until 1940, has already been mentioned. Many of the most famous authors and illustrators appeared in its pages, especially during the era of Mary Mapes Dodge, who was editor from the very first issue until her death in 1905.

One of the early successful children's publications in America was *Aunt Judy's Magazine*, which started in 1866 and was published for twenty years. Others were *Chatterbox* (1866-1943), *Little Corporal* (1865-75), *Little Folks* (1897-1926), *Merry's Museum* (1841-72), *Peter Parley's Magazine* (1833-44), and *Wide Awake* (1875-93). The earliest and by far one of the most popular for more than one hundred years was *The Youth's Companion*, which was founded in 1827 and survived

Reproductions of two of the illustrations for Beatrix Potter's *The Tale of Squirrel Nutkin.*

until the time of the stock market crash in 1929. Early editions of all these magazines are very rare and in some cases of considerable historical and sociological value.

One of the great phenomena to emerge from the publishing world of nineteenth-century America was the dime novel. It is said to have originated—at least in a commercial way—around 1860, when the Irwin P. Beadle Co. of New York City recognized the need for what was, in effect, a small magazine with only a single topic. The name obviously came from the cover price, 10 cents, and the fact that the contents were generally fictional or at least fictionalized fact. They owed their growing popularity to the Civil War, when soldiers could carry them handily in their rucksacks and trade them for other titles when they had been read.

From that time on, untold millions were sold, dramatizing the exploits of such heroes as Jesse James, Buffalo Bill, Frank Merriwell, Ned Buntline and the Horatio Alger boys. They continued in popularity until the latter half of the 1920's, when they began to be overshadowed by detective magazines and adventure publications featuring Tarzan, Doc Savage, Nick Carter, Captain Fury and The Shadow.

Series of books also became very popular after the turn of the century. These were not exactly dime novels but were usually very cheap editions, which boys and girls could purchase by saving up their allowances. The appeal was heightened by the fact that many educational authorities stated that they were trash, catered to lazy minds, and glorified impossible dreams. Furthermore, many parents, taking the advice of these warnings, tried to ban them from their homes and thus inadvertently promoted a huge underground market. Tom Swift, one of the greatest inventors and boy wonders in all fiction, was the idol of millions of young boys, who eagerly sought copies of each new title that appeared. The fun-loving, do-gooding Rover Boys also had an enormous following.

Although some of these volumes are valuable today, probably none can compare with the success story of that series of success stories, the Horatio Alger books. These were so much in demand during the period from the Civil War to the 1920's that more than sixty publishers issued reprints in the millions upon millions. Alger was one of the most prolific of all American authors, turning out no less than 107 full-length novels, as well as countless short stories and poems, before he died in 1899 at the age of sixty-five. Since most of the novels were originally published in serial form in magazines and newspapers, you can specialize in Alger and acquire pieces from all the media in which he appeared.

Reprints are not of great monetary value. Few command more than $10 or $12, and most are available for $1 or $2. But original editions, in mint condition, are so rare that you can seldom come by one for less than $30 or $40. If you are fortunate enough to own a copy of *Ragged Dick,* the story that launched Alger as a best-selling author in 1868, it may be worth upward of $250. *The Western Boy; or the Road to Success,* which was quoted at $50 just a few years ago, is said to have tripled in value since then. *Seeking His Fortune, and Other Dialogues,* published by A. K. Loring in 1875, is a curiosity. Although it was published in large quantity and is in fact a collaboration with Alger's sister, it is valued at about $400. Only ten copies are accounted for.

The Big Find, though, can only be *Timothy Crump's Ward; or the New Year's Loan,* published by Loring in 1866, before Alger was well known. Although it was simultaneously published in paperback and hard cover, only three copies are known to exist. Many were probably tossed out, even after Alger became famous and his works were highly sought after, because the author's name is not in evidence. Current value: more than $1,000.

Works like this obviously fall into the category of book collecting, which is a very complex and highly expensive field, which this guide could not even begin to cover. They are referred to mainly to show that collectors of modestly priced paper memorabilia and antiques should always be alert to items of great value that they *might* discover in the normal course of browsing. Let's say you suddenly realize that the value of a certain issue of an old magazine has risen rather dramatically in a short period of time. You might trace this to the increasing popularity of material by an author or illustrator in the issue. If so, look for a similar rise in value in hard-cover and paperback books by that author or illustrator.

The same could be true of subjects, such as fashion trends, historical events or personalities. Interest in original pieces from the Civil War period boomed at the time of the Centennial. Will the same be true of items from the Revolutionary War period as we draw closer to the Bicentennial in 1976? Who knows? Keep your eyes and ears open. Anniversary dates or the publication of nonfiction books that become best sellers

The cover of *All Story Magazine,* October, 1912.

will often be sufficient spark to generate a widespread demand for paper memorabilia relating to the people or events involved.

As in the case of children's magazines, cheap editions of books for the very young form a category that is easy to define and limit yourself to—if this subject has special appeal. Again, we are not talking about book collecting per se or first editions of *Alice in Wonderland,* but the kinds of popular publications that were but one step removed from magazines. The children's books of this type in the early nineteenth century make good collector's items because they were very small—only about 3″ x 5″, with sixteen, thirty-two or sixty-four pages. Some had advertising tie-ins or were at least used to help promote products peddled door to door by itinerant wagon salesmen. Some titles included stories about Red Riding Hood, Tom Thumb, Mother Hubbard, or Tommy Tucker. Others

VOL. I. [365] **The Boston Chronicle.** No. 41.

From MONDAY, SEPTEMBER, 19. to MONDAY, SEPTEMBER. 26. 1768.

ord Mansfield's Speech on WILKES Outlawry.

HAVE now gone thro' the ſeveral errors aſſigned by the defendant, and hich have been ingeniouſly argued, and nfidently relied on, by his counſel at e bar: I have given my ſentiments upon em, and if upon the whole, after the oſeſt attention to what has been ſaid, d with the ſtrongeſt inclination in favr of the defendant, no arguments hich have been urged, no caſes which ve been cited, no reaſons that occur me, are ſufficient to ſatisfy me in my nſcience and judgment, that this outry ſhould be reverſed, I am bound to rm it—and here let me make a pauſe. Many arguments have been ſuggeſted, h in and out of court, upon the conuences of eſtabliſhing this outlawry, er as they may affect the defendant n individual, or the public in geneas to the firſt, whatever they may be, defendant has brought them upon elf; they are inevitable conſequences aw ariſing from his own act, if the alty, to which he is thereby ſubjected, ore than a puniſhment adequate to crime he has committed, he ſhould have brought himſelf into this unnate predicament, by flying from uſtice of his country; he thought er to do ſo, and he muſt taſte the s of his own conduct, however bitter unpalatable they may be, and algh we may be heartily ſorry for any n who has brought himſelf into this tion, it is not in our power, God forſhould ever be in our power, to dehim from it; we can't prevent the nent of the law by creating irregu- in the proceedings; we can't pre- the conſequences of that judgment rdoning the crime; if the defen- has any pretenſions to mercy, thoſe nſions muſt be urged, and that exerciſed in another place where nſtitution has wiſely and neceſſarily it: the crown will judge for it- t does not belong to us to interfere puniſhment; we have only to de- he law; none of us had any con- n the proſecution of this buſineſs, y wiſhes upon the event of it; it t our fault that the defendant was uted for the libels upon which he en convicted; I took no ſhare in r place, in the meaſures which aken to proſecute him for one of it was not our fault that he was ed; it was not our fault that he t was not our fault that he was ed; it was not our fault that he rendered himſelf up to juſtice; none of us revived the proſecution againſt him; nor could any one of us ſtop that proſecution when it was revived; it is not our fault if there are not any errors upon the record, nor is it in our power to create any if there are none; we are bound by our oath and in our conſciences, to give ſuch a judgment as the law will warrant, and as our reaſon can approve; ſuch a judgment as we muſt ſtand or fall by, in the opinion of the preſent times, and of poſterity; in doing it, therefore, we muſt have regard to our reputation as honeſt men, and men of ſkill and knowledge competent to the ſtations we hold; no conſiderations whatſoever ſhould miſlead us from this great object, to which we ever ought, and, I truſt, ever ſhall direct our attention. But conſequences of a public nature, reaſons of ſtate, political ones, have been ſtrongly urged, (private annonymous letters ſent to me I ſhall paſs over) open avowed publications which have been judicially noticed, and may therefore be mentioned, have endeavoured to influence or intimidate the court, and ſo prevail upon us to trifle and prevaricate with God, our conſciences, and the public; it has been intimated that conſequences of a frightful nature will flow from the eſtabliſhment of this outlawry; it is ſaid the people expect the reverſal, that the temper of the times demand it, that the multitude will have it ſo, that the continuation of the outlawry in full force will not be endured, that the execution of the law upon the defendant will be reſiſted; theſe are arguments which will not weigh a feather with me. If inſurrection and rebellion are to follow our determination, we have not to anſwer for the conſequences, though we ſhould be the innocent cauſe—we can only ſay, *fiat juſtitia ruat cœlum*; we ſhall diſcarge our duty without expectations of approbation, or the apprehenſions of cenſure; if we are ſubjected to the latter unjuſtly, we muſt ſubmit to it; we can't prevent it; we will take care not to deſerve it. He muſt be a weak man indeed who can be ſtaggered by ſuch a conſideration.

The miſapprehenſion, or the miſrepreſentation of the ignorant or the wicked, the *mendax infamia*, which is the conſequence of both, are equally indifferent to, unworthy the attention of, and incapable of making any impreſſion on men of firmneſs and intrepidity.—Thoſe who imagine judges are capable of being influenced by ſuch unworthy, indirect means, moſt groſly deceive themſelves, and for my own part, I truſt that my temper, and the colour and conduct of my life, have cloathed me with a ſuit of armour to ſhield me from ſuch arrows. If I have ever ſupported the king's meaſures, if I have ever afforded any aſſiſtance to government, if I have diſcharged my duty as a public or private character, by endeavouring to preſerve pure and perfect the principles of the conſtitution, maintain unſullied the honour of the courts of juſtice, and, by an upright adminiſtration of, to give a due effect to, the laws, I have hitherto done it without any other gift or reward than that moſt pleaſing and moſt honourable one, the conſcientious conviction of doing what was right. I do not affect to ſcorn the opinion of mankind; I wiſh earneſtly for popularity, I will ſeek and will have popularity; but I will tell you how I will obtain it; I will have that popularity which follows, and not that which is run after. It's not the applauſe of a day, it's not the huzzas of thouſands, that can give a moment's ſatiſfaction to a rational being; that man's mind muſt indeed be a weak one, and his ambition of a moſt depraved ſort, who can be captivated by ſuch wretched allurements, or ſatisfied with ſuch momentary gratifications. I ſay with the Roman orator, and can ſay it with as much truth as he did, *Ego hoc animo ſemper fui, ut invidiam virtute partam, gloriam non infamiam, putarem*:" but the threats have been carried further, perſonal violence has been denounced, unleſs public humour be complied with; I do not fear ſuch threats, I don't believe there is any reaſon to fear them: it's not the genius of the worſt of men in the worſt of times to proceed to ſuch ſhocking extremities: but if ſuch an event ſhould happen, let it be ſo, even ſuch an event might be productive of wholeſome effects; ſuch a ſtroke might rouſe the better part of the nation from their lethargic condition to a ſtate of activity, to aſſert and execute the law, and puniſh the daring and impious hands which had violated it; and thoſe who now ſupinely behold the danger which threatens all liberty, from the moſt abandoned licentiouſneſs, might, by ſuch an event, be awakened to a ſenſe of their ſituation, as drunken men are ſometimes ſtunn'd into ſobriety. If the ſecurity of our perſons and our property, of all we hold dear and valuable, are to depend upon the caprice of a giddy multitude, or be at the diſpoſal of a giddy mob; if, in compliance with the humours and to appeaſe the clamours of thoſe, all civil

The front page of the Boston *Chronicle*, September 26, 1768. The eight-page paper contains news from the Massachusetts Bay Colony, "Charles-Town," South Carolina, and Quebec. One item covered the imprisonment of "one — — Neuman, for the murder of his father, a man of eighty years of age, by beating him in a most cruel manner."

were composed of puzzles, games, or conundrums. After color printing became commercially feasible, it was extensively used in children's books because of the special appeal to the young. The animal stories of Beatrix Potter (1866-1943) achieved great popularity, and early editions of her work are in demand by some collectors because she is still so popular among the young. The same can be said for Kate Greenaway and her marvelous illustrations.

If you are interested in art, don't overlook the early art instruction and drawing books. A specialist in the field of American primitive art reports that there were no fewer than one hundred different instruction books of this type issued in America between 1787 and 1860. These volumes, on subjects ranging from the elements of drawing to the art of flower painting and sketching the human figure, may be valued at as much as $150. Yet you can also acquire interesting examples for as little as 50 cents.

When collecting books and magazines, you must be especially careful to distinguish between originals and reproductions or at least know where to obtain an honest evaluation. There has been such a rash of reprints these days that it is almost impossible to keep up with the lists of titles. Just by way of example, a major publisher has recently come out with a series of reprints that include *The Police Gazette, The Youth's Companion, Phoney Phun,* and, of all things, *The Brooklyn Bridge Bulletin.* They cost $1.50 apiece.

For just $1, you can also purchase paperback reprints of *Mother Goose of Boston* (1830), *ABC Coloring Book* (1830), and *Uncle Frank's Animal Stories* (1870's).

What would you have to pay for originals at dealer's retail prices?

First, let's look at some rare newspapers:

Boston *Newsletter*, early issues from 1704 on, $75 to $100 per issue.

New York *Weekly Journal*, around the 1730's, $35 to $50.

Pennsylvania *Evening Post*, the issue of July 6, 1776, with the Declaration of Independence printed in the issue, as much as $500.

San Francisco *Chronicle*, May 7, 1937, with news of *Hindenburg* dirigible disaster, about $10.

New York *Dispatch*, 1880's, about $5.

Oakland *Tribune*, April 19, 1906, with news of San Francisco quake and fire, about $15.

New York *World*, 1880's, about $3.

Because most old newspapers are in fair to poor condition, that is a prime consideration in their value, next to rarity, age and subject.

Magazines are generally in better shape because they are by nature more durable. Here's what you would pay for some representative copies:

Godey's Lady's Book, 1860's, $10 to $20, depending on contents.

Scribner's Monthly, 1880's, $5.

Ladies' Home Journal, 1910, about $3, but double that with paper doll cutout sections.

Penny Magazine, 1833, about $10.

Peterson's Magazine, 1870's, about $10.

THE PENNY MAGAZINE

OF THE

Society for the Diffusion of Useful Knowledge.

87.] PUBLISHED EVERY SATURDAY. [August 10, 1833.

NEAPOLITAN MACCARONI-EATERS

[The Maccaroni Seller of Naples.]

Maccaroni, or maccheroni,—the learned are divided as to the orthography and etymology of the word,—is the principal food of the poorer, and the favourite dish of all classes of Neapolitans. So much is this the case that the people of Naples have had for many ages the nick-name of "Mangia-maccaroni," or maccaroni-eaters.

A fine English lady at Paris once asked a gentleman of her own country who had recently arrived from Italy, "On what sort of a tree maccaroni grew?" But, in all probability, most of our readers who have seen the substance do not partake of her ignorance, but know that it is made with wheaten flour.

"Grano duro," or "Grano del Mar Nero," the small, hard-grained wheat grown in the Russian territories on the Black Sea and shipped at Odessa and Taganrok, is considered the best for the purpose, and was once imported into Naples for the maccaroni manufacturers. As that kingdom is essentially agricultural itself, the importation of this foreign corn was felt as an evil; but as the manufacturers always declared they could not

Vol. II 2 R

The cover of *The Penny Magazine,* August 10, 1833.

"Les Modes Parisiennes," an Illman Brothers engraving from the March, 1861, issue of *Peterson's Magazine.*

Pulp magazines of the 1940's, such as *Startling Stories, Weird Tales, Amazing Stories* and *High Seas Adventure,* from $2 to about $6 each.

The Shadow Magazine, early 1930's, in fine or mint condition, $20.

The values of books can go into many thousands of dollars. But it might be helpful to cite a few of the more transient types and series that do not fall into the rare book category. Some examples:

Tarzan of the Apes, by Edgar Rice Burroughs, around $90; other books in the series up to $60 or $70.

Zane Grey books of the West, around $50 to $75.

Jesse James, My Father, a biography by Jesse E. James, about $80.

Paperback editions of movies, with pictures of stars, from $2 or $3 to $15 or more.

Early Tom Swift books, from $5 to $20, depending on subject and condition.

XVII

A Funny Thing to Collect

"Wow! There's a Kaboom in Old Comic Books!"

"EVER WONDER WHAT happened to those wonderful dime comics you used to swap with friends and ruin your eyes on during rainy Saturday afternoons?" asked *Changing Times* magazine in its January, 1972, issue. Going on to answer its own question, it reported that if you find any copies of the *Green Hornet, Captain Marvel* or the *Hawkman* gathering dust in your attic, "they may be collectors' items worth $5, $10, $50, sometimes much more."

There are estimated to be some 10,000 collectors of old comic books, and this does not take into account many others who collect related items, such as Buck Rogers "Solar System" maps that command $25, or T-shirts and mugs and pins and stickers and book covers with comic characters imprinted on them. The boom has been stimulated by a number of recent events that have helped turn onlookers into active participants. One was a convention in Washington, D.C., that attracted some 250 people interested in comic art. Another was what has become an annual event, the "Cavalcade of American Comics," sponsored by the Newspaper Comics Council, Inc., twelve newspaper syndicates and Sunday newspapers. The "Cavalcade" is centered on an exhibit of American comics, which is a history of comic strips from their beginnings in 1896.

You will also find that more and more museums and galleries are featuring the comics as a true art form and exhibiting the works of some of the masters, past and present, from the earliest illustrators to the more recent ones like the late Carl Anderson, Charles Schulz, Al Capp and Hal Foster. This kind of reception and recognition not only stimulates the interest of amateur collectors but helps mightily to upgrade the worth of items in this field.

Present-day comic books fall into ten categories, making it easy to specialize in one or several types:

1. Animated comic characters, such as Mickey Mouse, Donald Duck and others from Walt Disney.

2. Traditional comic strip characters, like Little Orphan Annie, Mutt and Jeff, and Blondie.

3. Westerns such as the Lone Ranger and Hopalong Cassidy.

4. Characters from motion picture series. Lassie is a good example.

5. Adult and older teen-age comics, with stories about romance, love secrets and confessions.

6. Detective stories, featuring characters like Dick Tracy.

7. Crime and horror stories, using Frankenstein-like monsters or gigantic insects from a prehistoric world.

8. Supernatural and superhuman figures, of which Superman and Batman are the prime examples.

9. War comics, using semihistorical tales from World War II or other wars and battles.

10. Pictorialized classics, adapted from the works of Charles Dickens, Robert Louis Stevenson and others.

The earliest examples of what is referred to as the modern comic are actually quite recent. Caricatures and other forms of comic art go far back in European and American history, largely as a medium for political and social satire. Although this, too, is an important field for many collectors, it is different from the one discussed in this chapter.

Another advantage, as you will see later, is that you will find many important and valuable pieces dating from barely thirty or forty years ago. A few, only twenty or twenty-five years old, are significant because of their particular place in the development of comics or because they represent some milestone in comic art.

"Newspaper comics as we know them today," says the Newspaper Comics Council, "trace their start to 1896, when an experiment in using yellow color on a press turned an otherwise unimportant figure into a comic favorite."

As it happened, an artist named Richard Outcault was burlesquing events of the day in a series of drawings he entitled *Down in Hogan's Alley*. These were very simple black-and-white sketches and used as one of the characters a boy with a bald head and big ears in a white nightshirt. When the paper started experimenting with the yellow color, Outcault talked the editors into letting him depict this figure in color instead of black and white, and *The Yellow Kid* was born. A further innovation was the writing of words on the nightshirt, instead of using brief captions at the bottom of the page.

The public was so delighted with the mischievous look and humorous sayings of the Kid that Outcault started a whole series. He really started achieving recognition, though, when a year or so later, he conceived *Buster Brown*, a name that has been a family word for almost seventy-five years.

Copies of turn-of-the-century newspapers featuring *The Yellow Kid* and *Buster Brown* are real collector's items. So too are the first issues in which a growing breed of comic characters began to appear. Among them were *The Katzenjammer Kids*, drawn by Rudolph Dirks and based on humorous illustrations brought back from Germany by William Randolph Hearst; George McManus' *Bringing Up Father*, which was the first of the family-situation comic strips; and Frederick Burr Opper's *Alphonse and Gaston*.

By the end of the first decade of the twentieth century comic strips were achieving great popularity and the public eagerly looked forward to the exploits of Abie the Agent, Mickey Finn,

Old Doc Yak, The Gumps, Happy Hooligan, Mutt and Jeff, Little Nemo, Hairbreadth Harry, Clarence the Cop and many others. The comics achieved something of an intellectual boost when *Krazy Kat*, the forerunner of comics devoted to social comment, was recognized as an example of art and not simply a funny illustration.

The comic book as a medium in its own right had its birth in 1911 in Chicago. By then newspapers had recognized the pulling power of comics in maintaining circulation and attracting new readers and were using them for various promotional purposes. Someone at the old Chicago *American* dreamed up the idea of using one of the most popular strips of the day, *Mutt and Jeff*, for this purpose. Consequently, readers who sent in coupons from certain daily issues of the paper received as a premium a pamphlet in which were published sequences from *Mutt and Jeff* comic strips. As you might suspect, this modest little publication, historic in its own right, is rare and valuable.

By the beginning of the 1920's many comic strips that are still well known were running in newspapers across the nation. They included *Tillie the Toiler, Barney Google, Skippy, Boob McNutt, Gasoline Alley, Winnie Winkle,* and *Popeye.* These were closely followed by *Smitty, Our Boarding House, Moon Mullins, Little Orphan Annie, Joe Palooka, Captain Easy*, and *Dick Tracy.*

Some collectors find a particular attraction in the artist who created a series of comic characters and will build their collections around him. One of the all-time greats was a man whose name is little known today outside the collectors' world. C. W. Kahles pioneered in the comic art and produced a number of significant firsts. His Hairbreadth Harry, started in 1906 in the Philadelphia *Press*, was the forerunner of the superhero. Many later artists owed to him the idea that a comic strip could be highly successful by depicting a hero endowed with special strength who was fighting against the forces of evil.

By the time he created Harry, Kahles had already proven

himself an innovator in his field. In 1900 he produced the first sequence about the police force, *Clarence the Cop*; in 1901 the first undersea adventure, *The Perils of Submarine Boating*; and in 1902 the first aviation strip, *Sandy Highflier, the Airship Man.* In a short biography of her father for *Good Old Days* magazine, Jesse Kahles Straut wrote: "His output was so prodigious that, according to one comic art collector, Ernest McGee, who has one of the world's largest collections, C. W. Kahles's production of successful comics may not have been equalled by any other cartoonist."

At one time, Kahles had seven strips running simultaneously in Sunday newspapers all over the country: *Billy Bounce, Clumsy Claude, The Teasers, Pretending Percy, Mr. Butt-In, The Adventures of Captain Fibb,* and *Clarence the Cop.* Kahles collectors also look for the many cartoons he drew for humor magazines like *Judge* and *Life*, for magazine and book illustrations, and for samples of his advertising art. He was a painter of considerable stature as well, selling landscapes, still lifes and portraits.

Had Kahles not died in 1931 at the age of fifty-three, he might have achieved great additional fame in the comic book field, which was to see an astonishing boom during the 1930's. Up until that era, comic books were relatively unknown. Their predecessors were probably the early game and riddle books, which had been popular as far back as the eighteenth century and which, during the Victorian Era, used cartoon-style illustrations. Many were compiled from series that had appeared in children's magazines like *St. Nicholas.*

In 1935 a comic-type magazine entitled *New Fun* began to appear on the market. It was followed soon after by a number of detective and action comics. These were the first continuing and commercially successful comic books with illustrations and plots specifically designed to fit the new format. Previous comic books, such as *Famous Funnies,* published in 1934 for the first time, and *Tip Top Comics,* 1936, were simply reprints of strips that had already appeared in newspapers.

The new medium was established in 1937, when *Detective*

Comics pioneered in telling one complete story. And the real thrust came when, in 1938, the superfamous Superman rocketed to fame and touched off dozens of imitators.

There are few fields of collecting where items of such recent vintage have soared so quickly in value. It is not at all uncommon to pay $5 to $10 for comic books in fine condition that were published just prior to 1940. And some are in the rare book class. For example, that first issue in which Superman appeared, *Action Comics*, issue Number 1, 1938, has a price tag of $200 to $300 or more (depending on condition). The first issue of *Detective Comics* in which Batman appeared, Number 27, May, 1939, is valued at $275.

Another graphic phenomenon of the 1930's was the *Big Little Books*. These were small, thick books with hard, though cheap, covers, which measured 4″ x 6″ in page size. There were two basic types of covers, often in color: comic art, depicting a cartoon hero or heroine; and photography, showing a scene and characters from a popular motion picture.

Most of the familiar comic characters appeared in one or more *Big Little Books*, including Little Orphan Annie, Jungle Jim, Flash Gordon, Mickey Mouse, Moon Mullins, Alley Oop, Buck Rogers, The Gumps, Donald Duck, Polly and Her Pals, Popeye, and Captain Midnight. In addition to most of the Walt Disney characters, Hollywood contributed such old faithfuls as Gene Autry, Tom Mix, Roy Rogers, Shirley Temple, Bambi and the Texas Rangers.

The *Big Little Books* were published in tremendous quantities, each one in the hundreds of thousands. Despite this great proliferation of copies, they are not as common as might be expected, especially in mint condition. The lesser ones go for $1 or $2, still not such a bad price when you consider that they were originally bought for only 10 cents or 25 cents. At a somewhat higher range, a spot check shows a listing of $5 to $7.50 for many editions (*Alley Oop, Donald Duck, Little Orphan Annie, Mickey Mouse, The Phantom, Tarzan, Tailspin Tommy, Terry and the Pirates*).

Among the more sought-after copies are Buck Rogers books,

which bring $12 or $15 and as much as $20 (*Buck Rogers and the Overturned World*); early Dick Tracy books (circa 1933), which are worth about $15; Jungle Jim, at $10 to $15; and the Flash Gordon series, from $10 to $20.

In the standard comic book field, you will find a much larger range of prices, including the very rare copies already mentioned. Surprisingly, some fairly recent editions have rocketed in value, a fact which suggests that comic book collectors should not overlook issues appearing after 1950 or even in the 1960's and 1970's. A recent magazine piece listed collectors who were looking for, among other items, the fifth issue of *Human Torch*, fall, 1941, at $25; the first issue of *Uncle Scrooge*, 1951, at $10; and the first issue of *Fantastic Four*, 1961, at $20.

Are these so desirable that their value will double by 1980 or at least go up considerably? Who knows? That is part of the excitement and stimulation of collecting. Prices can leap to a plateau and then remain there forever. They can also go *down* because the demands of the collector are not always predictable, and they are sometimes downright fickle.

Here are some further examples of what collectors are paying today for various examples of comic art:

1910 Buster Brown calendar	$ 7
1912 Kewpie Doll page from *Woman's Home Companion*	$4.50
Bringing Up Father, 1925	$14
Winnie Winkle comic book, 1931	$12.50
Ace Comics, issue Number 1, 1937	$60
Tailspin Tommy Adventure Magazine, late 1930's	$25

The cover of the first *Superman* magazine.
Copyright 1939 Detective Comics, Inc. Renewed © 1966 National Periodical Publications, Inc.

Rex King, 1941 . . . . $10

Captain Midnight, 1942 . . . . $25

Bambi, 1943 . . . . $15

Barney Google, 1939 . . . . $20

Captain and the Kids, 1938 . . . . $12.50

Felix the Cat, 1943 . . . . $10

Little Lulu, 1945 . . . . $6

XVIII

How to Make Worthless Documents Valuable

THERE IS A man on Long Island who makes a habit of seeking out worthless stock certificates for companies that have gone out of business. In the course of his meanderings, he has picked up such fancy items as some Imperial Russian government bonds that had a face value of $1,000 but were reduced to zero when the czarist regime was overthrown in 1919; stock certificates for railroads which became defunct as much as one hundred years ago; and fancy-looking securities for a collection of colorfully named gold, copper, silver and tin mines, many of which never produced any ore before their ultimate financial collapse.

A hardheaded businessman, he acquires collector's items at one price, evaluates them, and then sells them at a higher price. For considerable profit can be made in stock certificates for corporations long since liquidated, deeds to land that has been resold several times, or discharge papers of servicemen no longer living—to name just a few examples of "worthless" documents that accumulate value as part of a collection.

People who are interested in history often collect memorabilia of this type, along with other items relating to their fields of interest. Stock certificates are primarily curiosities, and very few have any great monetary value for the collector. For example, one current list from a dealer in the West, who specializes in mine and railroad documents, offers

NORTH BUTTE MINING COMPANY

600,000 SHARES

SHARES $15 EACH.

NUMBER 39376

SHARES 25

INCORPORATED UNDER THE LAWS OF THE STATE OF MINNESOTA

FULLY PAID AND NON ASSESSABLE

CAPITAL STOCK $9,000,000.

INCORPORATED UNDER THE LAWS OF THE STATE OF NEW YORK.

No.

SHARES

Oneida Railway Company

CAPITAL STOCK $15,000.

SHARES $50. EACH.

This Certifies, that ______ entitled to ______ Shares of the Capital Stock of the ONEIDA RAILWAY COMPANY, transferable only on the Books of the Company in person or by Attorney on surrender of this Certificate.

In Witness Whereof the said Company has caused its seal to be affixed and this Certificate to be signed by its President and Treasurer.

Oneida, N.Y. ______ 188__

Treasurer President

A stock certificate for the North Butte Mining Company of Minnesota. Shares were $15 each when this stock was sold in 1908. Shares for the Oneida Railway Company were $50 each in the 1880's.

individual items at prices ranging from 50 cents to $2, including stock certificates for the Utica, Clinton & Binghamton Railroad of the 1880's ($1.50); Lone Pine Surprise Mines of Washington, 1890's to 1930's (50 cents); Inland Brewing Company (50 cents); and Utica and Waterville Railroad, of the 1880's ($2).

Many certificates have great appeal because of their illustrations—old locomotives, mining scenes, street scenes with horse and buggies or horse-drawn streetcars, train tunnels, state buildings and seals, famous personalities and

Presidents, and smoke-belching factories. Many are well worth framing as conversation pieces. For this purpose, you can purchase complete sets of certificates, all in mint condition and unused. A Massachusetts dealer, for example, offers the following in an interesting illustrated catalogue: a collection of 87 different stock certificates and 24 bonds issued by railroad companies from 1850 to the early 1900's, along with several nonrailroad items, for $250; 42 different stock certificates from railroads of the same period, for $75; and a collection of 12 such railroad certificates, ornate, multicolored and with engraved vignettes, for $30.

One of the lures of collecting securities of this kind is that once in a blue moon they will suddenly retrieve something of their former value for the purpose for which they were originally intended. Discussing bonds issued by various governments, a financial publication pointed out that "there is no telling when, for reasons of international diplomacy or national image, a country may decide to make some settlement on its defaulted debt." Greece, Yugoslavia, Bolivia and the Congo were cited as nations that did just that, between 1964 and 1967, thus converting what many had considered permanently worthless paper into something of real value.

Since its formation in 1933, an organization known as the Foreign Bondholders Protective Council has helped negotiate restitution on more than $3.5 billion worth of formerly defaulted bonds from twenty-four countries. So if, in the course of seeking out specimens for your collection, you find that you can pick up some apparently valueless foreign bond certificates of this type for very little cost, it might just pay to do so—over and beyond the fun of having these in your collection.

No such windfall will result from collecting corporate stocks of companies that have gone out of business. Actually, not a few of these, especially in the really speculative fields like gold mining and gems, were fraudulent to begin with. They were beautifully engraved and decorated with scrollwork and

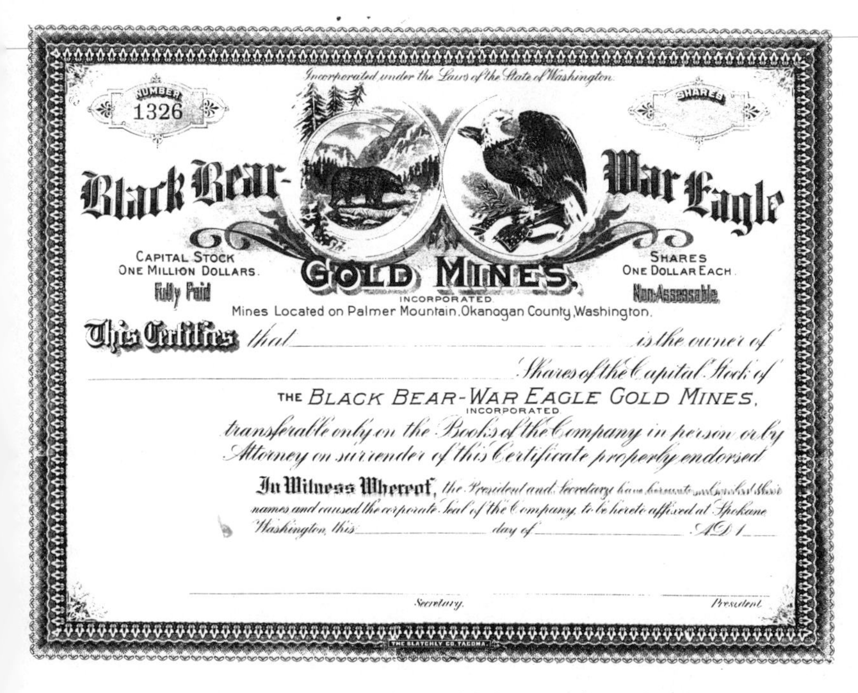

Incorporated under the Laws of the State of Washington

NUMBER 1326

SHARES

Black Bear-War Eagle

Gold Mines

Incorporated

Capital Stock One Million Dollars. Fully Paid

Shares One Dollar Each. Non-Assessable

Mines Located on Palmer Mountain, Okanogan County, Washington.

This Certifies that ______ is the owner of ______ Shares of the Capital Stock of THE BLACK BEAR-WAR EAGLE GOLD MINES, INCORPORATED, transferable only on the Books of the Company in person or by Attorney on surrender of this Certificate properly endorsed.

In Witness Whereof, the President and Secretary have hereunto subscribed their names and caused the corporate seal of the Company to be hereto affixed at Spokane Washington, this ______ day of ______ A.D. 1__

Secretary. President.

The Black Bear-War Eagle Gold Mines sold shares at $1 each. They might be worth considerably more today— as part of a collection of documents.

official-looking seals and sold for mere pennies by con men who roamed from town to town, luring buyers with the hope that they might just strike it rich. The peddlers then vanished, leaving a flood of worthless paper behind them.

Other documents that are interesting to collect are discharge papers, land grants, leases, sheriff's writs, and military orders. When starting a collection of this kind, a good approach is to buy representative samples from dealers until you have an idea about what is available and how much certain items are worth. Then you can start your own exploration by looking through attics, attending auctions, and trading with other collectors. The following are some examples of documents and current list prices if you buy them from dealers:

Revolutionary Pension Claim, 1836 . . . . $15

Troop provision document from the War of 1812	$24
Revolutionary War bounty land grant	$20
Confederate bond coupons	$3
Gold & King Mining Co. bond, 1883	$5
Confederate States mail service wayside bills	$10
Policy insuring American ship, 1794	$8
Parchment deed to South Carolina plantation, 1789	$20
Prohibition era whiskey prescription blank, with entries	$1.50
Bill of sale for slave, $500, 1844, Richmond, Virginia	$35
Wells Fargo draft, 1872	$8.50
Sheriff's writs, each	$3
Marine Corps discharge papers	$4

Although this book will not try to discuss in depth autograph collecting, which is a complex field unto itself, a few words here would be appropriate. Sometimes the value of an old document will be greatly increased because of one or more autographs on it. In the October 12, 1971, issue of *Antique Trader* Clarence T. Hubbard, an authority on this subject, wrote, "Autograph collecting today is at one of the highest points in history and the number of collectors is increasing."

With this kind of popularity, it is evident that such documents might have a two-fold interest (and value) for collectors.

Do not be deceived into thinking, though, that the value will be enormously increased just because the person is well known or famous. A number of factors enter the picture— the nature of the paper signed, the frequency with which the signer may have affixed his name to similar papers, and current interest in the person or subject matter. As Mr. Hubbard pointed out, a fine signature of our eleventh President, James Polk, on a white card recently fetched only $25. "But the letter former President Truman dispatched to the music critic who downgraded his daughter's singing is valued at $2,000 to $4,000."

Since a Truman signature generally brings only about $15 or $20, you can easily see that the nature of the document plays an important part in the value.

XIX

Leaping Back over the Years

YOU WOULD HAVE to look back thousands of years to find a time when there were no calendars of one sort or another. Scholars have spent lifetimes determining the origins of methods for keeping track of the days and nights and seasons. And if you were to look up the history of the calendar, you would find a proliferation of styles and types, as well as countless national, sociological, geographical, religious and other variations. You would read about the Gregorian calendar, the Christian Ecclesiastical, the Moslem, the Jewish, the Greek, the Roman, the Egyptian, and the New Style vs. the Old Style, among many other diverse subjects.

But don't think that you have to be an amateur historian to enjoy collecting calendars. Most collectors, with budgets too modest to dream of collecting works that are many centuries old, keep their hobby on a reasonable plane and are content to confine their collecting to specimens published within the past one hundred years or less, largely in the United States.

The calendar as we know it owes its origins to the Egyptians, who first worked out a system of twelve months for the solar year, a formula later adopted by the Romans. There have been numerous refinements since, largely to account for surplus days which did not fit into the months as defined by the Egyptians and the Romans. The calendar was still undergoing a change during the eighteenth century in America, which is why you frequently hear such statements as one claiming that George Washington was really born on February 11. This is true, since the Old Style calendar was in effect at the time of his birth and was not changed to the New Style until about twenty years later.

Some collectors not only limit their scope to the past one hundred years or less but also stay within a certain subject area, since there are literally hundreds upon hundreds to select from. These range from animals, plants, trees, fish and other nature subjects to antique cars, locomotives and trains, sports, architecture, fashions, personalities from the entertainment world, military and naval subjects, children, history, art—just about anything that suits your fancy.

Most people think in terms of wall calendars, which are rather large. But many collectors, especially those with limited space for storage and display, acquire only the smaller pocket or desk types. Then there are the aficionados of certain publishers, such as Currier & Ives, who have made a name in this field. Other collectors acquire any calendar they can locate and afford of certain artists who were prolific, such as Kate Greenaway, Rose O'Neill, Frederic Remington and, more recently, Rockwell Kent.

Almost since the beginning, the printed calendar has been a valuable advertising and promotion medium in America. But it began to reach its peak after 1870 when, along with almanacs and trading cards, it became a popular giveaway. One of its big advantages for advertisers was that a calendar was assured (once accepted) of a twelve-month life. It also gave the advertiser a chance to promote individual products, one month at a time, and was especially effective when using a seasonal approach.

It was therefore a natural for the manufacturers of patent medicines and other remedies. They could feature throat lozenges and cold syrups in the winter months, nostrums for poison ivy in the spring, salves for insect bites in the summer, and balms for aching muscles at the time of the fall harvest.

And all year round they touted pink pills for the liver, appetite stimulants and headache powders.

The manufacturers of household products also derived a great deal of mileage from calendars, which were usually hung in the kitchen— a handy place to display pictures of soap, pot scrubbers, lye, stove blacking, lamp wicks and the like. Some early calendars of this type are especially interesting, though not necessarily much more valuable, because of the notations scribbled on them from day to day and month to month.

Original calendars, whole and in fine condition, are not always easy to locate. For one thing, the users tended to rip off pages as the year progressed. Also, many of them were cut up and their illustrations used to decorate scrapbooks, letters or homemade greeting cards. Yet they are not expensive to collect. You can buy a Metropolitan Life Insurance calendar, circa 1908, for about $5, as well as an older one, 1892, for Clark's thread, showing a chubby baby's face bursting through a spool.

A St. Joseph's Oil Company calendar for 1884-85— all thirty-two pages of it— was recently listed at $4.50. And you can pick up calendars between 1900 and 1920 for $2 or $3, or up to $5 if they are colorful and in top condition.

XX

Where Do You Go from Here?

IF YOU HAVE always thought of maps as being merely practical and utilitarian, sit back and take a more relaxed look at the subject. They make marvelous subjects for the collector and can be of considerable educational value as well, without seeming to be homework in any sense of the word.

One of the most cherished maps in one collector's treasure, however, would not inform a living soul about how to get anywhere. It was published in very limited quantity as a promotion piece for L. Frank Baum's childhood masterpiece, *Wonderful World of Oz*, first published in 1900. In glowing colors and whimsical illustrations, it depicts a warm, bright land of Nowhere.

In general, map collecting can be highly informative, helping the owner understand the world better, as well as learn fascinating facts about historical events that brought about changes on the maps. As a collector, you can start at any level you choose, acquiring a map for a mere pittance or investing small, modest or large sums in maps and charts that have established values as real antiques. The best way to start is by collecting mainly for the fun of it, selecting specific regions that particularly interest you, rather than ranging the world. You would be surprised to find how many items you could locate that relate just to your own state, county or even community.

Bear in mind that the category also includes charts of rivers, lakes, bays, sounds and other bodies of water; surveyor's projections; city plans; relief maps and topographical sketches; military battle layouts; population patterns; political boundaries; rainfall distribution and climate zones; highway and road maps; landforms; time zone charts; and a variety of other graphic formats providing information on additional subjects, from vegetation and underground waters to celestial bodies, agriculture, wildlife, trails and footpaths, and many other measurable physical, geological or cultural features.

The types that interest most collectors, though, are the decorative wall maps that are pleasurable to look at and that also have enough detail to make them fascinating to study. Very often, you can locate an old atlas that is in poor condition on the exterior but has insert maps that are well preserved. This kind of find might cost $10 or $12 but yield twenty or more good maps that have a resale value of $1 or more each. When making this kind of purchase, however, select only those atlases which have insert maps printed on one side only. Some may also have foldout maps, though generally these are not as desirable as similar ones without creases. If you buy an atlas which is complete and in excellent condition on the exterior, be hesitant about removing pages until you have kept it for a while and are certain the parts separately are worth more than the whole intact.

Authentic old maps have a special charm, especially those that have been lovingly embellished with dolphins, griffins, cherubs puffing out their cheeks to blow favorable winds to the bellying sails of galleons, and heraldic emblems. Many early map makers used the very practical device of filling up gaps that had not been charted yet in detail with illustrations of savages, treasure chests and sea fights. Later copies tended to overdo the pictorial elements, often with the effect of being too crowded to be of any practical use.

Collectors of old navigation charts try to obtain ones that have been used for specific voyages and that contain an exact

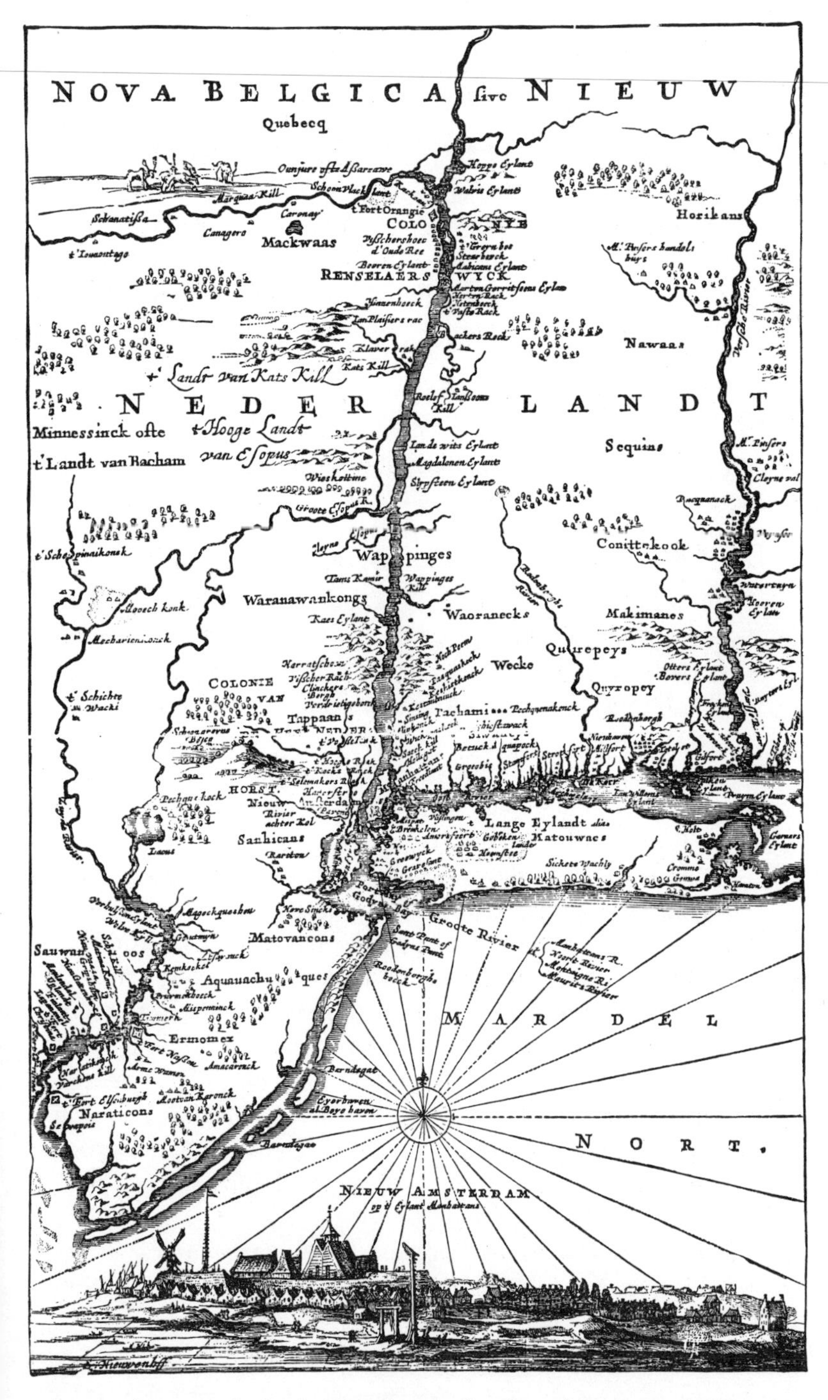

A map of New Netherland, 1656, shows a drawing of the town of Nieuw Amsterdam at the bottom.

record of where the ship has sailed. These are fascinating to trace. And if you are fortunate enough to locate one for a famous ship or a historic voyage, you may have a real discovery on your hands. Charts for the American clipper and whaling ships of the last century are good examples, though rare indeed. After all, it required some two years for a whaling ship to complete its circuit and return with its hold filled with valuable oil.

Many of the individual elements in maps are of great interest, and some actually help establish the date, origin and authenticity of a particular map. If you go in for collecting, you will quickly become familiar with these units, of which the following are characteristic examples:

Border. Since the shape of the area being depicted is never regular and often very ungainly and lopsided, the border serves a strong decorative purpose. It helps the eye encompass the area covered more easily. The arrangement of elements within the map helps balance the design artistically within the border.

Layout. This refers to all the elements, including the border, their arrangement in relation to each other, size and degree of visual emphasis.

Scales. Every map has one or more scales, showing how many miles equal an inch. Many maps also interpret this in terms of kilometers or other units of measurement. And several show two or more different units, especially when there is a variation in usage among the countries included in the map.

Cartouche. This is a box or panel, usually decorative, without the border, which contains the title of the map and other necessary information. Some cartouches are simple, being no more than lines, while others are elaborately ornamented with scrolls, entwined leaves, knotted ropes, figures, emblems and other artwork.

Inset. Many maps have insets, which occupy space that would otherwise be empty. Insets commonly show a close-up of a city plan in a scale larger than the rest of the map or details of the entrance to a harbor.

Legend. Columns of symbols, located in or near the element containing the title, are explained in brief captions. A typical legend might use such symbols to pinpoint the location of docks, churches, government buildings, navigational signals, and other subjects vital to effective use of the map.

Vignette. Decorative maps make extensive use of vignettes, which are nothing more than sketches of people, scenes, events and other subjects positioned in appropriate places and so rendered that they seem a part of the map itself.

Heraldry. Many old maps make colorful use of coats of arms, banners, flags and similar units that quickly identify the government(s) having jurisdiction over the areas depicted on the map. Many of these will be unfamiliar to you at first, since the countries or governments have changed or been taken over by other powers.

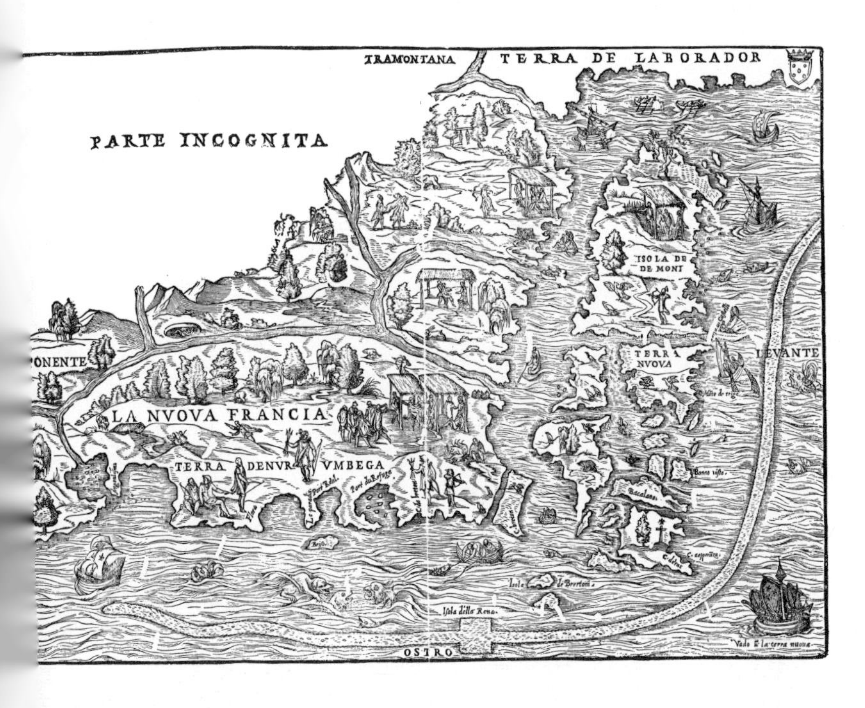

A fanciful map of "La Nvova Francia" shows figures, sailing ships and imaginatively drawn fish.

Collecting and studying maps in chronological order is an informative and stimulating way of bolstering your knowledge of both geography and history.

Many people who acquire maps also start complementary collections of guidebooks, particularly the paperback type, which usually contain maps as well as detailed facts. Such guides go back to about the middle of the nineteenth century, but they did not reach a height of popularity until the 1870's and 1880's, when printing processes made it possible to publish cheap editions in mass quantities, with color illustrations of local scenes and people. Motoring guides became popular after the turn of the century, as soon as traveling by automobile became feasible in America. You can locate copies of these guidebooks, showing various cities and points of interest and containing street maps, for about $5, for an issue published before World War I.

Souvenir photo albums interest some map collectors, particularly if they are focusing their attention on maps of cities. These are inexpensive. For example, you could pick up guides for $3 to $5 showing Boston in 1900; Coronado Beach, California, in 1899; Saint Augustine, Florida, in 1913; Washington, D.C., at the end of the last century; and Niagara Falls in 1906.

The prices for maps themselves vary a great deal, depending on many of the factors that affect other types of paper antiques and memorabilia: condition, rarity, age, subject, quality and size. If you want to consider map collecting as an investment and are willing to go back two hundred years in American history, you might think seriously about specializing in the Revolutionary War period. Maps and charts published prior to, during, and just after this era are certain to increase strongly in value (assuming they have some value to begin with) as the nation approaches the Bicentennial in 1976. Bear in mind, though, that other collectors will have the same objective in mind. So if you take this route, make it your first point of order to seek out some of the less obvious sources of such material.

XXI

Fashions, Fads and Paper Dolls

THE OCTOBER 15, 1904, issue of the old *Collier's* magazine has double value as a collector's item. First, as one of the most popular and significant periodicals of its time, it is sought after by collectors of magazines. Second, but of prime importance to the subject of fashions, it represents a milestone in the history of American clothing. For this is the "Gibson Number," with twenty drawings and a double page by Charles Dana Gibson, creator of an American dream that became a reality, the Gibson Girl.

Although artists and writers throughout history have established ideals of beauty and dress and personality that have captured public attention and influenced styles, no one has ever topped Gibson in the degree to which he changed the entire course of social history in America.

Born in 1867, the artist attended the Art Students' League in New York City at the age of eighteen and soon began selling sketches to the humorous weekly *Life.* He was successful enough to be asked to join the staff of the magazine, where he first began sketching what was to become known as the Gibson Girl. These early sketches, showing beautiful young ladies in various wholesome activities, particularly out of doors, are of great interest to collectors. Gibson's art became so popular that he was eventually commissioned by *Collier's* to produce fifty-two weekly drawings for the magazine's centerfold at a total

COLLIER'S

"DANGEROUS!"

Title page of *Collier's* October 15, 1904, issue, the famous "Gibson Number," featuring drawings by Charles Dana Gibson.

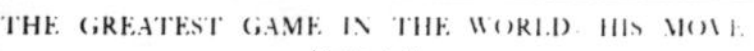

Four previously published Gibson drawings, as reproduced in the special Gibson issue of *Collier's.*

price of $50,000. It was the largest amount ever paid to a magazine illustrator up to that time, on any basis. These illustrations were not all girls, by any means, but covered a wide range of situations, both with humor and with a rare social understanding.

Some collectors specialize in Gibson and his era. They have a wider range of selection than you might imagine, since Gibson contributed to *Century, Harper's, Scribner's* and most of the other major magazines, illustrated books, was a highly successful painter, and even influenced the theatrical world. Collectors can find Gibsoniana on old calendars (and recent ones, too), postcards, posters, advertising literature, playbills, playing cards, fashion prints, doll cutouts, valentines, trading cards, sheet music and many other forms of memorabilia that people like to collect.

Although the Gibson Girl reached her peak of popularity and cultural influence at the end of the last century, her beauty, personality and expressiveness have such a timeless quality that she has strongly influenced every succeeding generation. It is no wonder that Gibsons, in any form, are so collectible!

Another great name in American fashions that has long fascinated collectors is *Godey's.*

Louis Antoine Godey was born in New York City in 1804. In 1830, at the age of twenty-six, he and a partner founded a modest magazine, which they entitled simply *The Lady's Book.* The name was changed to *Godey's Lady's Book* after the partner withdrew from the venture and became what has been called "the first successful woman's magazine." Early issues of the original publication and the ones at the time the name was changed are rare and valuable.

What appealed to collectors long ago, as well as to those today, were the remarkable full-color illustrations of ladies' fashions that appeared in the magazine shortly before the founder's death in 1878 and continued on, issue after issue. Godey's illustrations were not static, as had been earlier ones in other magazines. They not only depicted fashions à la mode but showed the wearer in all her glory: at the opera in off-the-shoulder numbers, taking tea in an elegant drawing room, strolling with handsome gentlemen in the park, on boating cruises, or riding to hounds.

Such fashion plates were originally hand-colored lithographs, often influenced directly by Paris, which was then, as recently, the center of fashion design.

Godey's was not the only magazine with these fashion plates and an enormous appeal to a female audience. Another close contender was *Peterson's Magazine,* along with *Demorest's* and *The Delineator.* A collection of these publications shows graphically the changing styles and trends in clothing. When *Godey's* was first established, women were wearing many underskirts. The mid 1850's marked the appearance of

A color "fashion plate" from *Godey's Lady's Book*, showing the latest styles for January, 1868.

crinoline, a stiff material which belled out the skirts without requiring the weight of all those underskirts. In issues of the 1860's, you can see the crinoline effect gradually being pushed out of style as the famous bustle literally mushroomed its way into fashion.

Single prints that were extracted from these magazines are not always easy to find. The best ones will cost $5 or more. Yet just a few years ago collectors were able to purchase entire volumes of *Godey's,* intact and with a dozen such prints, for from $10 to $15. Unfortunately, the market has jumped astonishingly fast. A recent offer quoted an 1849 copy of *Godey's* at $60, an 1866 issue at $40, and an 1855 *Peterson's* at $75.

Are these prices typical? Not necessarily, for the issues in question not only contained a number of excellent lithographs in black-and-white and in sepia but also sheet music, either for piano or guitar and voice. When adding to your own collection, look for multiple treasures like these, which add to the value and interest of the periodical. Many magazines also carried paper doll cutouts in certain issues, which are highly prized by some collectors (as will be discussed later).

Many collectors are thankful for the suggestion made by a tailor's wife, just before the Civil War, in Sterling, Massachusetts. Why, she asked her husband, couldn't there be patterns available for women like the ones he used to make clothes for his customers? The husband, Ebenezer Butterick, was a man of an enterprising turn of mind. And in 1864 he opened an office at 192 Broadway in New York City, where he made and sold patterns, at first largely for children's clothing. The idea flourished, and it became the basis for a whole new American industry. Early paper patterns and sketches of ladies' fashions related to the patterns are good collectibles for people interested in this subject. Handmade stencils and templates are also included.

Before you start this kind of collection, though, bear in mind that such patterns are not too easy to store or display. They are

Children's fashions were illustrated in charming prints like this one from *Peterson's Magazine.*

"Early Spring Street Styles" from *The Delineator,* March, 1902, were shown in color.

usually fragile, require careful handling, and when spread out to see take up quite a bit of space. One collector has solved the problem by taking photographs of each pattern he acquires. He stores the patterns in large plastic envelopes and keeps the photos (5″ x 7″) in a convenient album.

PAPER DOLLS

In the year 1280, the Venetian explorer Marco Polo reported that paper figures of human beings were used in ancient Chinese and Japanese religious rites. It was a long time, though, after this before the Western world took to paper dolls. As far as the amateur collector is concerned, paper dolls did not really have much meaning until the middle of the eighteenth century, when the French discovered *pantins*, paper figures named after the district in Paris where they originated.

The appeal of the *pantins* lay in the fact that they were often life-size and were invariably made in sections, with joints. Through the use of connecting strings, the head, torso, lower arms, upper arms, thighs and legs could be made to move separately or in rhythm. The resultant antics were just what appealed to the French sense of humor and verve. The jumping jack toy is a miniature version of the *pantin*, with the same kind of enduring appeal to many ages.

Not until early in the nineteenth century did the paper doll as we think of it appear on the American scene. Dolls were first sold in England, then in Germany and France, printed on sheets of flat paper, which also included various changes of costume. Some were hand-painted in color, while others were black and white, leaving it up to the buyer to do the coloring. All had to be cut out, using shears or knives.

Paper doll sets prior to 1800 are very rare, especially those that are still in an uncut condition.

During the first decade of the nineteenth century, publishers experimented with a new idea: pasting envelopes or pockets in

Reproduction of a cover of *Dolly's Dressmaker, a* book of patterns published by Raphael Tuck and Sons, Ltd., "Publishers to the Queen," in 1896.

children's books, each containing paper doll characters from the text. They did not catch on readily, so books of this type are difficult to locate.

Not until 1854 did any American publisher feel that the paper doll had commercial possibilities. That year Crosby, Nichols & Company of Boston published a booklet of verses and a doll named Fanny Gray, packaged in a box, which also contained a wooden base for the paper figure and several changes of dress. *Godey's Lady's Book* adopted the idea in 1859, publishing an entire series—six girls and six boys—with costumes representing the latest in young fashions. Issues with these dolls are hard to find, especially with the figures uncut and intact and an 1859 issue of *Godey's Lady's Book* containing all twelve color plates would cost about $50 today, more if in mint condition.

One of the most successful producers of paper dolls was Rafael Tuck and Company, Ltd., of London, which also had an office in New York and was noted as an early publisher of picture and greeting cards. Many people specialize in Tuck

Dolly Dingle as she appeared in *Pictorial Review,* December, 1921.

dolls, along with a few others, because of their reputation for color, detail and high-quality paper. The Tuck firm, which published a famous series that included Martha Washington and "Six Famous Queens," may well have sparked the fad for dolls representing famous personalities. Not only royalty, but famous stage personalities like Jenny Lind, Maude Adams, Geraldine Farrar, and Shirley Temple all have been portrayed as tiny paper figures at one time or another.

Magazines and newspapers quickly followed the trend, some creating their own special characters as a means of appealing to the loyalty of readers and to keep them buying the publication. You will find that the old *Ladies' Home Journal* had an entire household called the Lettie Lane Paper Family; *The Delineator* had its Adele; *Pictorial Review* touted its waiflike Dotty Dingle; and Betsy McCall can still be found in the pages of *McCall's.*

The *Woman's Home Companion* went all out with Punch

A reproduction of Rose O'Neill's charming Kewpies.

and Judy, The Twins That Never Grow Older and the Kewpies. The last-mentioned set off a stampede of collectors, and even today, more than half a century later, have a cult of admirers. As *Mid-American Reporter* said in an article by Rowena Godding Ruggles in March, 1972, "The words 'Rose O'Neill' and 'Kewpie' have been synonymous for over half a century. Today the Kewpie dolls and drawings evoke feelings of nostalgia among collectors of old and antique dolls in all parts of the country. Interest has grown to such proportions that a group in Branson, Mo., has formed the National Rose O'Neill Club to establish a lasting memorial to this artist, author and poet."

The Kewpie was born in the *Ladies' Home Journal* issue of December, 1909, in the form of drawings and first appeared as a paper doll in the October, 1912, *Woman's Home Companion.* Two years later, the Kewpies had their own hard-cover paper doll book, the first of many. They had already appeared, in 1910 and 1913, as sketches in *The Kewpies and Dotty Darling* and *The Kewpies: Their Book.*

Collector's items all!

Among the easiest paper dolls to begin collecting are those which were created for advertising purposes, since there was a great proliferation of these and many are still to be found. Palmer Cox's Brownies, to mention one subject still familiar to many people, were used as premiums in doll form to promote Lion coffee. They were used as inserts on cardboard, appearing right in the package, as were dolls for a competing brand, McLaughlin's coffee. Other dolls helped sell as diverse a range of products as Clark's thread, Worcester salt, Duplex corsets, Bull Durham tobacco, Enameline stove polish, Singer sewing machines, Columbia bicycles, Aunt Jemima pancake flour, Diamond dyes, and William A. Rogers silverware. Some dolls were associated only with one product or brand, while others were used by two or more advertisers to sell noncompeting products, as were the Worcester salt dolls, which were also offered by a manufacturer of thread.

Paper dolls became so popular that they were big business for a number of companies that specialized in paper products. The Dennison Company enthusiastically entered this field in the 1890's, when it became commercially feasible to print figures in four-color and die-cut them or perforate them in large quantities. Interestingly enough, the catalogues published by Dennison are so rare that you can seldom find copies outside museums or rare book collections. If you should ever come across one in reasonably good condition, snatch it up at almost any price!

One of the fascinating aspects of collecting paper dolls is that you can find a wide enough range to appeal to almost any age. And they range in size from less than an inch to six feet or more in height. The life-size figures are a great curiosity, and nobody seems to have a good explanation as to why they were made. They represent soldiers, shepherds, lovely ladies, boys and girls (sometimes playing with dogs, cats or pet birds), housemaids sweeping or dusting, and policemen, among many other subjects. One theory is that they were placed in the rooms and corridors of large mansions in Europe simply to provide companionship for the live inhabitants. Another theory is that they were placed in conspicuous positions near windows or in yards to thwart trespassers or burglars.

You will find a number of male collectors of paper dolls. They are more interested, though, in the military subjects, sports figures, or the types that were once commonly used as actors and actresses for miniature theaters, also made of paper or cardboard. You will also find a multitude of paper scenes and settings to go with the nontheatrical dolls. These include such items as paper houses, furniture, groves of trees, motorcars, early airplanes, shops, castles, forts, ships, trains, military weapons, windmills, and covered wagons.

As you can well imagine, prices and values vary immensely, depending on the subject, condition, age, coloring, rarity and other factors. Since dolls were so often parts of series or sets, it is also important to consider the completeness of these. A family of paper dolls with setting, clothing and accessories would obviously be of much greater value, as well as interest, than just the figures alone.

Here are some characteristic values:

Sheet of three different ballet ladies of 1890's. $7.50

Set of three prints of ladies' heads, with hats and ostrich plumes, circa 1900 . . . . $1.50

Three "bloomer" ladies, circa 1890 . . . . $6

Godey's Lady's Book paper doll cutouts, from edition of 1859 . . . . $12.50

Ladies' Home Journal, with paper doll sheets, issues from 1908 to 1918, each $6

Set of 25 Spanish-American War soldier dolls, 6 inches high, on bases $25

Raphael Tuck 9-inch doll, with four costumes, series 23A $30

Similar Tuck doll, with four costumes and four hats $35

Set of 12 Worcester salt dolls, with costumes $18

Recent uncut paper dolls in mint condition, Tricia Nixon, Connie Francis, Pat Boone, Jane Russell, each $2.50

XXII

Some Sticky Matters

> If the contents of this bottle do not cure whooping cough, palsy or coughs within three days, your money will be cheerfully refunded.
>
> Guaranteed to remove freckles painlessly.
>
> Contains a secret ingredient passed down by an Indian Chief and known only to the Manufacturer.
>
> Contains Opium and Morphine for FULL EFFECT, but is *Non-Habit Forming*.

COLLECTING OLD LABELS, particularly from patent medicine bottles and pillboxes, can be as humorous as it is fascinating. The claims are often unbelievable, the language flamboyant, the names rib-tickling. Did you know that there actually *was* a Kickapoo Indian potion, along with others whose names resemble something out of a W. C. Fields movie at its best? These include La Dore's Bust Food, Dismal Swamp Chill and Fever Tonic, and Dr. Williams' Pink Pills for Pale People. That it was common for manufacturers in the late nineteenth century to tout their wares as "Good for man or beast"? Or that some medicine producers went out of their way to label their "cures" as containing upward of 90 percent alcohol? Finding and mounting the labels from products like these can be an amusing and rewarding hobby.

Since just about every product under the sun was labeled in one way or another, the nature of your collection is limited only by the subjects you want to cover. In addition to medicinal products, others that have highly collectible labels are food products, soft drinks, liquors, beer, clothing, furniture and furnishings, tobacco, hardware items, knitting and sewing supplies, stationery, perfumes and toiletries, paints and varnishes, and household cleaning supplies.

You will come across old labels in a number of ways. Trading between collectors is one of the most frequent methods of acquisition and disposal, and you will find offers in the various collecting, hobby and antique periodicals. Dealers also offer labels in advertisements, sometimes in packages of a dozen or more unused labels. Among some recent pricings were: a packet of five cigar box labels for $3; "Genuine Pre-Prohibition Beer Labels," four for $1; fifty assorted tobacco labels from cigars, cigarettes, chewing tobacco, snuff, etc., many with colorful illustrations, $10; a collection of old patent medicine labels, all in color, ten pieces for $4.50; and large liquor bottle labels from around 1900, 50 cents each (buyer pays postage for orders under $5).

How do you know these are originals rather than reprints (of which there are many in existence)? Since it is very difficult for the amateur hobbyist to tell the difference between original (old), which is usually brittle and hard to handle, and reprint (new), the best policy is to make purchases only from dealers whose reputations you can trust.

Many labels are found right on the product—on old bottles, food tins, boxes or bags. They are relatively easy to remove, undamaged, by steaming them. But then the question arises: Is the label worth *more* while still affixed to the container? If so, is it worth that much more to *you*, since it requires additional storage space? Only time, experience and your own interests will determine the answer.

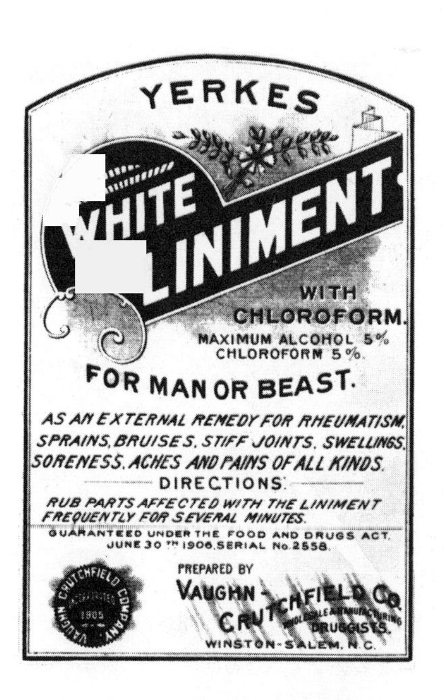

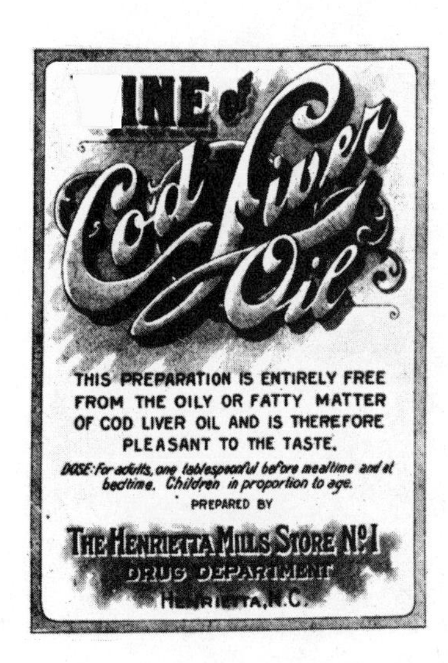

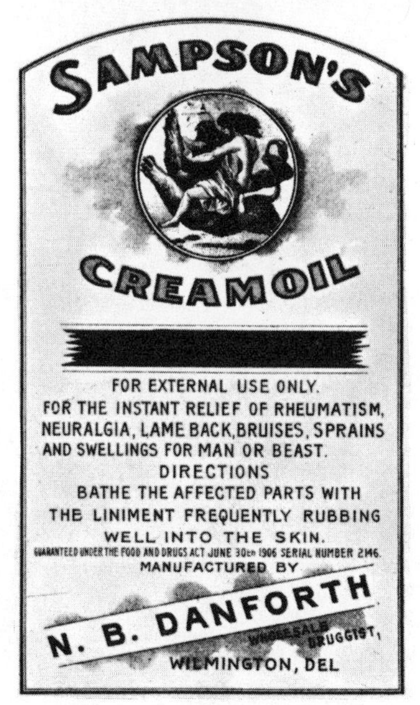

Labels for various remedies as advertised in the catalogue of H. Gamse & Bro., manufacturers of druggists' labels and boxes.

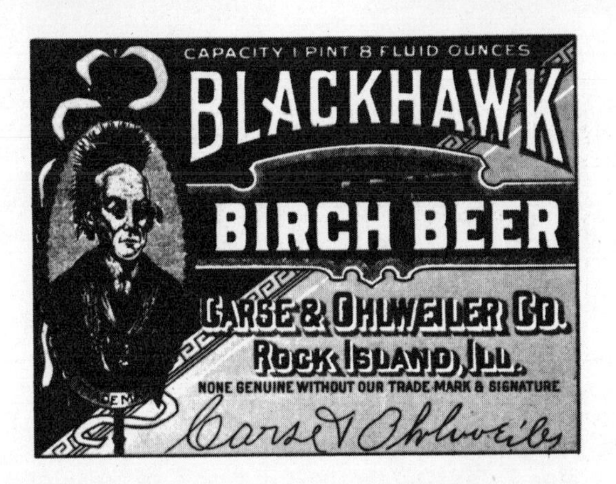

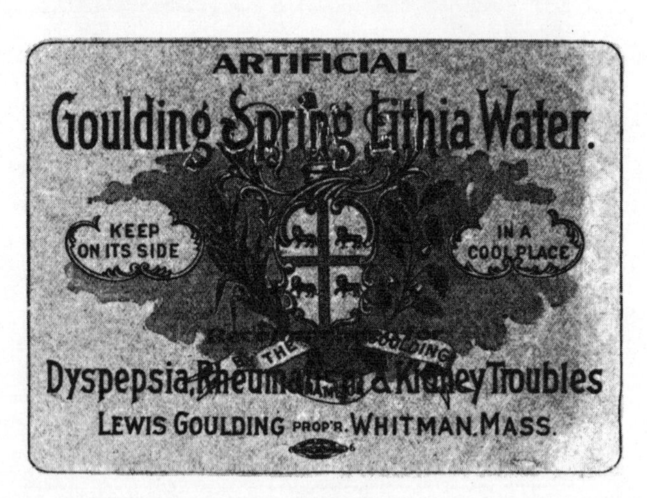

Labels for a variety of products are interesting and easily acquired paper collectible

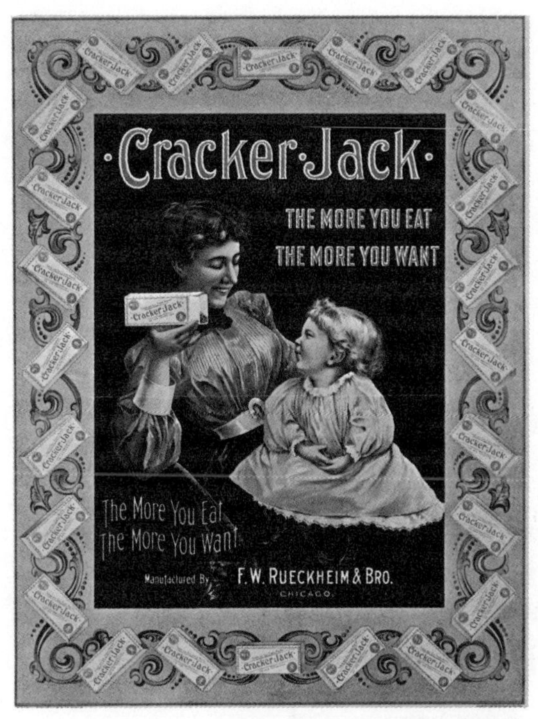

Photo by John Rilke Bayalis

A label from a tin of Cracker Jacks, 1902.

Many collectors specialize in one field, either by type of product, historical period, geographical location, manufacturer—or a combination of two or more of these factors. But for the beginner, the best plan is usually to start collecting everything you come across that interests you. Unlike many collectibles, labels are small, easy to store, well suited for colorful display, and inexpensive to acquire. Also, you can start with items of more recent vintage, which cost little but could go up in value with time, and then work your way back to the real antiques.

As you proceed, you will find that certain groups are highly desired. For example, any that are associated with the Shakers of two or three generations ago—or longer—are in demand. The Shakers grew and packed many vegetable products, put up jellies, jams and other preserves in jars, and packaged flower and vegetable seeds. Since the labels for many of these products were hand-printed, in limited quantities, they are among the rarer items.

Old labels with pictures are of special interest not only for their graphic qualities, but because the illustrations help establish their date of publication. Perhaps even more important, they make marvelous displays as tiny, colorful vignettes of past eras. Typical ones show maids serving bowls of steaming soup; factories with smoke pouring out of tall stacks (environmentalists, take note!); and children drinking beverages with obvious delight.

When mounting labels for display, do not use glue or paste or any adhesive that may still be on the back of the labels. If you are mounting them in albums or scrapbooks, the use of photo corners is convenient, holds the items with reasonable security, and avoids damage to the exhibits. If you make up wall displays, labels can be secured to the mountings by using stamp hinges, those tiny, gummed bits of paper that stamp collectors use and which will not devalue the items displayed.

Properly collected, mounted, and displayed by subject, period, location or other category, each individual label acquires a great deal more value, granted that the collection is extensive enough and significant enough to be of real interest to collectors. You will learn to tell the difference between labels for a specific product that seem to look alike. There may be subtle changes in color or design that to the eye of an experienced person mark one acquisition as ten or twenty years older than a similar one. Since label collectors almost invariably buy duplicates from time to time for trading purposes, it is important to become aware of these tiny shades of difference. And whenever you have a chance to buy an entire lot of labels (as perhaps at an auction of items from a warehouse), consider the value of such a purchase for trading purposes. Yet never buy in quantity in this manner unless you are reasonably sure that you will be picking up something you can really use for trading.

While not considered labels in the pure sense of the word, travel stickers are also of interest to many people who collect labels. While the older ones, with colorful, antiquated illustrations, are the rarest and most valuable, collectors always keep their eyes open for items from little-known and seldom-visited countries. Especially valuable are those representing countries that were short-lived, even though fairly recent, such as the African nations that have come and gone so quickly in recent years.

In a similar manner, you will find more interest in hotels, airlines, steamship companies and locations that hardly anyone has ever heard of than in subjects representing familiar, well-beaten paths.

"I try for 'impossible' combinations," says one successful collector. "I am constantly looking for examples from countries, cities and regions that are little known. Then if I can also find stickers from tiny hotels and inns in those countries, as well as an airline or railroad or midget boat line, I really have a package of great value and fascination.

"Suppose you were collecting labels and I offered you a set consisting of three travel stickers for the Republic of Mali; several for hotels in Timbuktu and Bamako; and a couple for the Niger and Senegal River Steamboat Line— all in that same small West African nation—your eyes would light up! Unfortunately, I don't have any, and I'm not sure that Mali even has a steamship line. But this is the kind of combination I'm constantly seeking out. And that's what makes collecting such rare good fun."

BOOKPLATES

It is natural for the collector of labels, travel stickers and the like to have an interest, too, in bookplates. Since they are in the same size range, they can be collected, arranged and displayed in similar fashion.

There is one enormous difference, however, between these

otherwise-comparable collectibles. Whereas labels and promotional stickers were printed in the thousands, even millions, bookplates are almost one-of-a-kind items. You may come across a package of unused bookplates, one hundred or more in all. Yet you will probably never find that same plate again. And if you locate old copies individually or remove them from books that are otherwise of no value, the chances are very slim that you will ever find more than just the single copies so acquired.

Most bookplates have very little monetary value and are prized more as curiosities or because of unusual pictures or quaint phraseology. Yet there are some that are not only rare but extremely valuable, especially if they bear the names of famous authors, statesmen, artists or other personalities. Look particularly for those that are signed or that may have a handwritten notation. Some antique marks go back many centuries and are real museum pieces. Others that are of recent vintage may have high price tags because they bear the names of famous men who were great collectors of books, such as Winston Churchill, Franklin Delano Roosevelt or Ernest Hemingway.

Signed bookplates also come under the category of autographs and are sold as such by autograph dealers.

Another type which is rare, interesting and highly collectible is the handmade bookmark. Most that you will find are in the primitive tradition of American art, with crude illustrations, sentimental inscriptions and the owner's name in very fancy lettering. Again, there are a few that are worth a great deal that were devised by famous people, especially in the creative fields. Especially prized are examples sketched by people in their youth, long before they became famous.

Bookmarks represent a companion field, although you will not locate many examples of note that were made of paper. A popular type one hundred years or so ago was the Stevengraph, which was not made of paper at all, but of silk. It fits the paper category, however, since it was often mounted on cardboard.

The Stevengraphs were so called since they were made by the Thomas Steven Company of Coventry, England, in the mid-1800's. They were marked "woven in silk by Thomas Stevens." They were pictures made on a Jacquard loom and were sold in the thousands at exhibitions such as New York Crystal Palace Columbia Exposition and Centennial and at stores that sold fancy goods. They were made in several widths, but the most popular were the narrow ones which were used as bookmarks.

There were many who imitated the original and these were called Textilographs. They, too, were made on the Jacquard look and used as bookmarks. They, too, had various designs on them as well as Christmas cards, mottoes, etc.

Bookmarks of this kind, especially those that were sold at the New York Crystal Palace Exposition, 1853-54, and the Philadelphia Centennial Exposition in 1876, are rare and valuable. You would pay, for instance, about $75 for one with a picture of the Crystal Palace, about $30 for a common scene like stagecoaches making a run, and perhaps $40 for a historical scene showing the landing of Columbus in the New World.

Paper bookmarks are inexpensive. Those with an advertising message, from the 1880's, are easily found for $1 or less. Illustrated ones on heavy paper or cardboard with personal names range from 50 cents to perhaps $3 or $4. Of course, if you find one with a famous name and perhaps a handwritten inscription, it could have considerable value.

As you can see from the foregoing discussion, collecting labels, bookmarks and travel stickers is both practical and entertaining for collectors who have little storage and display room, the desire to explore numerous fields and periods, and limited budgets.

XXIII

And in Conclusion

Have postcards of Maine, Mass., N.H., pre-1920 scenes to swap for Connecticut lighthouses. . . .

Candy Bar Wrappers. I believe people will collect *anything*. Have old family album containing 20 pressed candy wrappers of early Twenties. It's yours for $2 and I promise not to tell who bought it!

Postcard Lotto. Early card game in original box, with tiny postcards having round-the-world scenes. All for $20.

Old cardboard litho *Railroad Scenery*, never cut and still in orig. boxes. I have 3 sets. Each: $4.25.

Advertising Checkerboard, promoting Banner Lye. This does not want for color. Fine condition. Circa 1895, 12″ x 12″. . . $17.50.

Want Buck Rogers and Tom Mix stuff. Have Gibson Girl prints, small books, old *Saturday Evening Posts*, Box A 656, N.Y.

Have 50 sets of old sheet music (1900-1940), also music

Glossary

Advertising Card: See Trade Card.

Almanac: Booklet issued by a particular business firm. The booklets were free and distributed in order to amass a huge audience. They contained jokes, puzzles, superstitions, dreams or sayings. *True Almanac:* This booklet was usually issued by a business firm or sold by publishing firms. It was a yearly calendar giving the days, weeks, and months of the year, weather forecasts, astronomical information, times of high and low tides and other tabulated data.

Aquatint: Plate covered with porous material through which acid penetrates to pockmark the metal. When printed in colors, the colors are rubbed into the plate wherever they are to appear in the print.

Big Little Book: Small, thick book with hard, though cheap, cover, which measured 4″x 6″in page size. This was most popular in the 1930's.

Bookplate: A printed label, often having a design, pasted in a book to indicate ownership.

Broadside: Formerly, a large sheet of paper printed on one side announcing some fact. Often used to announce coming entertainment to a community.

Brownie: Created by Palmer Cox and found in poems and stories created by Palmer Cox. The Brownie was a mischievous but helpful spirit who came out of hiding at night to accomplish some task left over from the workday.

Bubble Gum Card: Insert card found in a bubble gum package. Topics were sport figures, naval vessels, airplanes, trains, cars, and other timely material that would be of interest to young people. Cards are still issued by various manufacturers of gums.

Calling Card: A small card, printed or engraved with one's name, used to announce a visit or call; also called a visiting card.

Carte de Visite: Same as calling card.

Christmas Card: The exchange of cards at Christmastime began in England, and the first one is believed to have been designed by J. C. Horsley, R.A., in 1843 and lithographed by Sir Henry Cole.

Church & Dwight Card: Card inserted in Church & Dwight baking soda which was well printed with faithful reproductions of birds, fish, dogs, other animals, and flowers.

Cigarette Picture: Picture of a stage favorite, ballplayer, pugilist, or other notable that was enclosed in packages of cigarettes 1880-1900; for example, in Sweet Caporal packages. It was the forerunner of the bubble gum card.

Collage: A picture, partly painted and partly made up of cut paper and tinsel work glued to it.

Color Print: Colored from a single plate, which necessitates painting between each printing, or colored from several plates, which permits greater uniformity in the impression.

Comic Strip: A strip of cartoons printed in newspapers or other periodicals that relates adventurous or comic stories.

Comic: See Comic Strip.

Condition: The state of a particular piece, which is an important consideration in determining the value. The categories are:

Mint: Any object so designated is like new, has no wear or tear or other defects caused by handling, and has retained much of its original color and finish.

Fine: Object so designated is in excellent condition with perhaps a few signs of wear.

Good: Object so designated is in average condition.

Fair: Object so designated has noticeable signs of use.

Poor: Object so designated is noticeably damaged or incomplete.

Cutwork: Paper cut into fancy designs to form patterns and pictures.

Decal: See Decalcomania.

Decalcomania: Designs printed on a thin film of gelatin, mounted on paper, that can be transferred from the paper, by moistening, to any other surface.

Divided Back Card: Postcard with a picture on one side, with a line down the middle of the back of the card. The left side is for the message and the right side for the address.

Etching: A process of engraving in which lines are scratched with a needle on a plate covered with wax or other coating, and the parts exposed are subjected to the corrosive action of an acid; a figure or design formed by etching.

Folio: A paper size used generally to designate sizes of prints or pictures:

Small Folio: 11″ x 14″ to 11″ x 17″.
Medium Folio: 14″ x 18″ to 15″ x 20″.
Large Folio: 19″ x 24″ to 23″ x 27″.

Greeting Card: An ornamental card with complimentary greetings celebrating birthdays, holidays, etc.

Handbill: A printed advertisement or notice usually distributed by hand.

Impression: A term applied to any print made from a metal plate, wood block, or stone.

Label: A slip of paper, a strip of cloth, a printed legend, etc., on a container or article showing its nature, producer, destination, or other pertinent information.

Lithograph: A print produced by the process of lithography—that is, from a flat stone or zinc or aluminum plate on which a drawing or design has been made in a greasy or water-repellent material.

Mail-Order Catalogue: A publication containing articles for sale issued by a business enterprise by mail.

Map: A representation on a plane surface of any region, as of the earth's surface; a chart.

Mezzotint: A method of engraving in which the roughened surface of a copper or steel plate is scraped or burnished to produce effects of light and shade; a print produced from such a plate.

Navigation Chart: A special type of map which contains an exact record of where a ship has sailed.

Pantins: Type of paper doll made in sections with joints. Through the use of connecting strings, the head, torso, lower arms, upper arms, thighs and legs could be made to move separately or in rhythm.

Paper Doll: Doll that is made of paper to be cut out. The doll comes in either booklet or sheet form. Each doll has costumes.

Paper Filigree: See Quillwork.

Paper Toy: Various types of toys lithographed on heavy paper or cardboard to be cut out or punched out and folded to form a toy; for example, a castle with soldiers or a dollhouse with furniture.

Pattern: Anything shaped or designed to serve as a model or guide in making an item such as a piece of clothing.

Playbill: A bill or poster advertising a play; a program of a play.

Playing Card: One of a pack of cards used in playing various games; the pack consists of 52 cards divided into four suits (spades, hearts, diamonds, clubs) of 13 cards each.

Postal Card: A card, issued officially, for carrying a written or printed message through the mails under government stamp.

Postcard: A postal card; an unofficial card of any regulation size, usually having a picture on the front side, sent through the mails at the same rate of postage as a postal card.

Poster: A placard or bill used for advertising, public information, etc., to be posted on a wall or other surface.

Premium Booklet: Booklet distributed by various business firms to the buyer of the product; it was usually free and ranged in subject matter from nursery rhymes to puzzles, nature studies, dream interpretations, recipes, and fortune-telling. Firm's name was very prominently displayed throughout the booklet, or else the material in the booklet was slanted to include the firm's name very frequently.

Print: An impression produced from engraved blocks, metal plates, stone or other materials and which can be reproduced in quantity.

Pulp Magazine: A magazine printed on rough, unglazed paper, usually having contents of a sensational nature.

Quillwork: Paper strips about 1/8″ wide, fluted, twisted, or rolled into tight little scrolls which are then arranged in designs closely resembling mosaic work.

Sheet Music: Music printed on unbound sheets of paper; especially, music for popular songs.

Silhouette: A profile drawing or portrait having its outline filled in with uniform color, commonly black, and often cut out of paper. It was named after Étienne de Silhouette, France's finance minister in 1757, who instituted so many petty economies that anything cheap was called à la Silhouette.

Steel Engraving: The art and process of engraving on a steel plate; the impression made from such a plate.

Stereoscope Card: Card used on a stereoscope. The card contains two pictures of an object each seen from a slightly different perspective, which when viewed through the stereoscope blend into one image, giving an impression of three dimensions.

Stevengraph: Woven picture made on a Jacquard loom by Thomas Stevens of Coventry, England. Thousands of these pictures were sold at the various large exhibitions in the second half of the nineteenth century.

Sunbonnet Babies: Created by Bertha L. Corbett. They were little children in long skirts and huge bonnets, and they were drawn without faces. Used on all sorts of merchandise.

Tarot: One of a set of playing cards with grilled or checkered backs used in Italy, as early as the fourteenth century, by fortune-tellers and gypsies in foretelling future events.

Textilograph: Jacquard-loomed ribbon picture similar to Stevengraph but not made by Thomas Stevens. Used in bookmarks, Christmas cards, mottoes, to depict Mother Goose characters and others.

Theater Program: See Playbill.

Trade Card: A business card or advertising card; originally a small cardboard stating only a man's name, business and address and later usually illustrated with colored lithographs of the firm's building or trade or else a print that had absolutely no relationship to the business advertised.

Trade Catalogue: Booklet sent out by a merchant to advertise his wares, usually containing a picture, description, and price for each of the items he sold. From these catalogues, the customer selected the merchandise he wanted and sent the order to the merchant.

Woodcutting: An engraved block of wood or a print made from such a block.

Wood Engraving: The art of cutting designs on wood for printing; the making of woodcuts. A block so engraved or a print taken from the block.

Wood Print: See Woodcutting.

Index

Index